Co

Lo

Chicago

(If you're ever in
the neighborhood like!)

All the best
— take care

A

(see p ?? for where we
live !!)

Coffee Lover's Chicago

COFFEE SHOP GUIDEBOOK AND JAVA JOURNAL

Edited by
Sarah Burgundy

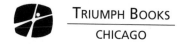

TRIUMPH BOOKS
CHICAGO

This book is available in quantity at special discounts for your group or organization. For further information, contact:
Triumph Books
644 South Clark Street
Chicago, Illinois 60605
(312) 939-3330 FAX (312) 663-3557

ISBN 1-57243-110-5

Cover design and illustration by Mark Anderson.

Triumph Books and its researchers have endeavored to make this listing as complete as possible and cannot take responsibility for errors of fact or omissions. Corrections and additions are welcome at the above address.

Contents

Acknowledgments

Special thanks to Geeta Nathan for bringing so much diligence and enthusiasm to this project and for drinking so much coffee.

Also thanks to Jeff Arner, Garrick Beil, Siobhan Drummond, Virginia Evans, Barbara Fillon, Joe Kleinschmidt, Jacob Mayfield, and Jennifer Ritsema for your invaluable assistance.

Introduction

You've seen articles about them in *Business Week* and *Newsweek*. Students study endlessly at their tables, they set the stage for television shows, they offer entertainment on a par with bars, and such terms as *latte* and *half-caf* are no longer foreign or jargon. Coffee shops have found their niche.

There are now 200 plus coffeehouses in Chicago, and more are opening every week. Although many are the somewhat uniform chains, familiar and reliable, huge numbers of creative, innovative shops are following suit. It's more than the coffee; each new place creates an atmosphere, whether grungy, sterile, alternative, classy, global, or cozy. When we began this project, we expected it to be a challenge to differentiate the shops. As it turned out, the real challenge was finding two alike.

Each review gives you a comprehensive guide to the atmosphere each shop offers. We avoided rating the coffee itself; everyone has their own preferences. Instead, we looked to whether the place was quiet or lively, how it was furnished, whether smoking is permitted, outside seating in the summer, and any other notable characteristics. Some coffeehouses make great local hangouts, while others are worth a trip to visit.

We had to draw the line somewhere, so we left out shops that don't serve espresso drinks (with a couple of notable exceptions) as well as restaurants (even if they do serve espresso) and other types of businesses whose main focus is not to provide the ultimate in java. We also eliminated carts located in mall food courts and building lobbies. In the case of chains or multiple locations, we most often list locations under one entry.

How to Read the Directory Listing

Our imaginary coffee house:

Kaffe Klatch	Name
1234 N. Anyplace	Address
North	Neighborhood
(312) 555-5555	Phone number
M-Su 7 A.M.-10 P.M.	Hours

rating (☕ is poor, ☕☕☕☕☕ is great)

$$$ price ($ is cheap, $$$$ is expensive)

smoking is permitted or smoking section is available

there is seating outdoors in nice weather

couches are a seating option

there is artwork on display

live music is offered

live reading of poetry, comedy, skits, and performance art

table games are available

there are books to read

beer and/or wine is served

In other words, Koffee Klatch has it all: board games, a huge library of books, live music on the weekends, a selection of beer and wine, and some of the best lattes in town. Prices are low, the portions are huge, and they offer space for a large crowd and cozy couches to curl up on for a quiet read. The brightly painted walls create a festive neighborhood coffee shop. This would be a true find.

The Coupon Passport

Once you've scoped out the directory, it's your turn to visit the shops. You'll find over $75 in offers from a number of the coffee shops in this book. Each shop will stamp their coupon when you redeem the offer. We've even left some space for you to take notes. Your Coupon Passport and Java Journal then becomes a record of where you've been and what you thought of them.

For more help, check the indexes to locate the closest cup of coffee, or the most reasonable, or the one that's still open, or. . . .

We wish you a wild, wonderful tour of Chicago's coffee shops.

Directory of Coffee Shops

A Note about the Ratings

Ratings range from five cups (highest) to one cup (lowest). Please take into account that most of the ratings were based on a single visit, and that, in any case, they are subjective.

Artist's Cafe

412 S. Michigan Ave.
South Loop
(312) 939-7855
Su-Th 6:30 A.M.-11 P.M., F-Sa 6:30 A.M.-12:30 A.M.

$$$$

With a wide selection of meals, desserts, and coffee drinks, the Artist's Cafe makes for a good visit after a movie at the Fine Arts Theater. The food is good, although the names often display more imagination than the dishes; a Capone burger is simply a patty with marinara sauce and mozzarella. The drinks are often large, rich, and expensive. Be warned: they have a $3 minimum per table as well. However, the atmosphere is fun and boisterous, so if you're looking for a good place to chat, you've found it.

Atomic Cafe

6746 N. Sheridan Rd.
Far North
(312) 764-9988
Su-Th 7:30 A.M.-12 A.M., F-Sa 7:30 A.M.-2 A.M.

$$1/2

A decidedly college crowd frequents this modern-looking Rogers Park cafe. With lamps on the tables and lots of space, the

Atomic is great for reading, talking, or playing a game of chess with one of the regulars. The menu is somewhat typical, but the food and coffee consistently taste wonderful. Located next to a discount movie theater, the Atomic is a perfect stop before or after a good film. See coupon on page 110.

au bon pain

180 W. Jackson
South Loop
(312) 341-0828
M-F 6 A.M.-6 P.M.

$$$

Au bon pain caters to the commuter in for the morning coffee. A banklike maze leads customers to the counter, where the employees work in an assembly line production. The decor and menu are typical, although the food is extremely fresh. They bake on premises and offer vegetarian, low-sodium, and low-fat foods. In addition, au bon pain has a policy of donating leftover items to food shelters at the day's end. Despite the high price, this is a good place to take out a cup of coffee.

Other locations:
181 W. Madison, South Loop
200 W. Adams, South Loop (312) 419-7570
78 E. Adams, South Loop
180 N. Michigan, Loop (312) 419-1629
222 N. LaSalle Ave, South Loop (312) 419-0450

Bean Counter Cafe

1/2

1932 Central St.
Evanston
(847) 332-1116
M-Th 7 A.M.-10 P.M., F-Sa 7 A.M.-12 A.M., Su 9 A.M.-9 P.M.

$$

The Bean Counter offers a full range of $2-$3 foods from breakfast to dessert, along with extensive coffee drinks. The spacious cafe offers a large picture window, tables scattered at different levels, and couches. One of the few family cafes, they also stock plastic children's seats. With enough space to escape any smoke or noise, innovative art, and live entertainment, the Bean Counter offers something for everyone. See coupon on page 111.

Bean Post

2404 W. Lunt Ave.
Far North
(312) 338-7700
M-F 7 A.M.-12 P.M. and 6 P.M.-8 P.M., Sa-Su 8 A.M.-3 P.M.

$$

The Bean Post is a small neighborhood shop that does mostly takeout business. Although there are a few tables for seating, it's not a great place to sit. However, they offer a nice selection of beans, coffee-making accessories, tea, and cups. The latte was somewhat bitter, while the service is particularly friendly and personal in this six-year-old shop that fills a niche in West Rogers Park. See coupon on page 112.

Beanie's Coffee & Tea Shoppe
1949 E. 71st St.
South Side
(312) 241-7699
M-Sa 7:30 A.M.-2 P.M., Su 8 A.M.-12 P.M.

$

This South Side shop appears a bit run down, but it's a good neighborhood stop next to the University Park Metra. The coffee and light breakfast items are extremely inexpensive and appear fresh, and the service is very friendly. They open their doors Sunday afternoons April though June for poetry readings, and the tall, colorful seats get lots of sunlight for reading. Beanie's is a good stop if you're in the area.

Other location:
7150 S. Exchange Ave., South Side (312) 734-7699. See coupon on page 113.

Beverly Bean
2734 W. 111th St.
South Side
(312) 239-6688
M-F 6 A.M.-3 P.M., Sa-Su 7 A.M.-3 P.M.

$$

Just like a little home, Beverly Bean welcomes the close-knit local community and genial outsiders alike. With fresh pastries and a selection of five to six coffees daily, this shop also offers creative espresso drinks, whole bean coffee, and loose leaf teas. With tablecloths on every table, handmade craft decor, and friendly chatter, this is a fine place to catch up with an old friend or make some new ones. See coupon on page 114.

Bittersweet   1/2
1114 W. Belmont Ave.
North
(312) 929-1100
Tu-Su 7 A.M.-7 P.M. (closed Mondays)

$$

The perfect complement to coffee's bitterness is a sweet dessert, and Bittersweet presents this combination perfectly. Award-winning owner/chef Judy Contino prepares some of the richest, tastiest desserts in the city; they also offer sandwiches and soups for lunch. The white tables and walls give this small shop a bright glow, and fresh flowers on the round marble tables add to the cheerful atmosphere. It can grow loud due to its size, so it's not ideal for reading, but the moderate prices, outstanding desserts, and soothing atmosphere make Bittersweet a must.

Borders Coffee Shop
822 N. Michigan Ave.
Near North
(312) 573-0564
M-Th 8 A.M.-10 P.M., F-Sa 8 A.M.-11 P.M., Su 11 A.M.-8 P.M.

$$

The coffee shop on the second floor of Borders Books and Music attempts to recreate coffeehouse atmosphere with a permanently painted chalkboard behind the counter. It has a nice seating area with large picture windows and flowers on the tables. They offer the basics in drinks and light fare. The iced latte is a little watery, but otherwise the food and drinks are fine.

Other location:
2817 N. Clark St., North (312) 935-3909

Boudin Bakery Cafe
900 N. Michigan Ave.
Near North
(312) 649-3570
Su-Th 8 A.M.-8 P.M., F-Sa 8 A.M.-9 P.M.

$$1/2

Located within the Bloomingdales building, Boudin freshly bakes their croissants, muffins, and breads daily. The counters are confusing—it's not obvious where to order—but once you do order, you can sit in the large seating area inside and a stylized "outdoor" area in the mall. The service isn't particularly friendly, but the foods are fresh, and you can overhear some juicy conversation from nearby tables. See coupon on page 115.

Bourgeois Pig!

738 W. Fullerton Ave.
North
(312) 883-JAVA
M-F 6:30 A.M.-11 P.M., Sa 8 A.M.-12 A.M., Su 8 A.M.-11 P.M.

$$$

With an interior of worn wood and blackboards describing the numerous offerings, the framed portraits and black marble tables of the Bourgeois Pig! come together in a decidedly comfortable atmosphere. They feature live alternative music and jazz periodically, hot coffee, cold coffee, and caffeine-free drinks, as well as an eclectic menu of soups, salads, and pastries. Books and games are available to patrons, who mostly consist of DePaul students and Children's Hospital employees, and the service is casual and friendly. See coupon on page 116.

Brewster's Coffee Co. 1/2

161 N. Clark St.
Loop
(312) 759-2811
M-F 6 A.M.-6 P.M. (closed Saturdays and Sundays)

$$

This tiny corner shop on Clark Street offers excellent coffee at reasonable prices. Although its size doesn't permit eating in, they have outdoor tables in the summer. A few nice touches, including fresh zucchini bread and genuinely friendly service, give this chain a comfortable feel.

Other locations:
300 S. Riverside Plaza, Loop (312) 559-0791
211 E. Ohio St., River North (312) 245-9930
    (open weekends, 7 A.M.-4 P.M.)

Brother's Gourmet Coffee
2800 N. Clark St.
North
(312) 549-4434
M-F 7 A.M.-9 P.M., Sa 7 A.M.-9 P.M., Su 8 A.M.-8 P.M.

$$

This corner shop at Clark and Diversey has competition from five cafes within a half block; however, Brother's may have the edge. With window seats and tables, they offer seating that the other chains won't accommodate. The coffee sizes are also large and cost less than average without sacrificing quality. Large vacuum-sealed canisters protect the whole beans from oxygen, thereby keeping them fresher. This shop also has small brown lamps that add warmth to the chain look.

Other locations:
2 N. Michigan Ave., South Loop (312) 630-1133
6441 N. Sheridan Rd., Far North (312) 262-3002

Cafe Ambiance   1/2
822 Clark St.
Evanston
(847) 328-4848
Daily 11 A.M.-1:30 A.M.

$

This dimly lit shop seems to hold little charm for a visitor on
first glance, but the Evanston establishment will grow on you.
By day slightly bland, at night the air becomes smoky, the music
plays louder, and students flock in with homework and gossip.
The coffee isn't necessarily the best in town, but it is passable
and inexpensive, and they offer a handful of desserts. While in
Evanston, Ambiance is a fine, fun place to find yourself.

Cafe Avanti
3706 N. Southport Ave.
North
(312) 880-5959
Daily 7 A.M.-12 A.M.

$$

Cafe Avanti features a small counter with crowded tables, but it has a quaint charm. Note the art on display, the water bowl and complimentary dog biscuits for canine visitors, and the extremely friendly and businesslike service. Although they do not bake their own foods, everything is fresh, particularly the cookies, which are big enough to make a meal. This is an excellent place to read a book or talk about the film you saw at the Music Box. See coupon on page 117.

Cafe Cafina
1588 N. Milwaukee Ave.
West
(312) 227-8400
Daily 7 A.M.-7 P.M.

$$

Cafe Cafina is a small corner shop with industrial decor—shiny black floor, silver metal countertops, and green and rust walls. The only seats are eight stools along a window. They also have a window to the street for quick takeout orders. The food and coffees are good, although they list only their drinks on the menu above the counter. Cafina is worth a quick stop on the way to the train. See coupon on page 118.

Cafe Cappuccino

3719 N. Harlem Ave.
Northwest
(312) 736-3521
Daily 8 A.M.-2 A.M.

$$

For a true Italian experience and, not surprisingly, some of the best coffee in town, try Cafe Cappuccino in the heart of Little Italy. This is not a place to cozy up with a book; you will find mostly Italian spoken here, several beers on tap, and a somewhat odd decor. However, their espressos are truly Italian in body and quality, the price is right, and the neighborhood is a bit of an adventure.

Cafe de Casa

400 N. State St.
River North
(312) 527-5916
M-F 7 A.M.-5 P.M., Sa 10 A.M.-5 P.M. (closed Sundays)

$$

Run by a father and his two sons, Cafe de Casa adds a nice touch to River North. With a glass front, tile entry, hardwood floor, exposed brick, whitewashed walls, blond wood tables, and a concrete counter, the interior is a pleasant infusion of different materials. Stop in at lunch for a variety of sandwiches, all for under $5, or try some of the pastries, including a sour cherry brownie or a cranberry pistachio biscotti. The Torrefazione Italia coffee is perfect for an afternoon escape.

Café Equinox

2300 N. Lincoln Ave.
North
(312) 477-5126
M-F 7 A.M.-12 P.M.; Sa-Su 7 A.M.-1 A.M.

$$$

Advertised as "Chicago's most beautiful cafe," Equinox gladly boasts its extensive history: once an ice cream parlor, it served Capone, Dilinger, and Chaplin. Designed by Louis Sullivan, it still has the original marble booths and tables. With books lining the walls and intense chess matches, Equinox draws a fair share of DePaul students. They're known for their cappuccino with honey over ice, vegetarian chili, homemade soups, and salad dressings. The coffee is too strong for some, and the desserts may be too rich for others, but Equinox is a definite crowd-pleaser.

Cafe Express

615 Dempster St.
Evanston
(847) 864-1868
M-F 7 A.M.-11 P.M., Sa 7:30 A.M.- 11 P.M., Su 8 A.M.-4 P.M.

$$$

This long, narrow shop has lots of surprises for a new visitor. One small room has bags of whole beans; visit it for the wonderful smell. If the tables along the windows are full, try the spacious back room. A latte with flavoring and a scone costs $4. The scones are small but tasty, while the lattes are extremely strong—a regular is equivalent to a double. However, the server can adjust the drink to your taste. Good for reading or talking.

Cafe Express South

500 Main St.
Evanston
(847) 328-7940
M-F 7 A.M.-11 P.M., Sa 7:30 A.M.-11 P.M., Su 8 A.M.-7 P.M.

$$$

A more spacious sister to the Dempster Street location, Cafe Express South offers more room to spread out with reading, writing, or talking. The coffee here is also extremely strong, and the food is very fresh. The atmosphere is classic cafe: intellectual and serious, and they prove you can still find a cup of regular coffee for under $1.

If the horseshoe sinks, then drink it.
—Plains recipe for coffee

Cafe Josephine   1/2

711 N. State St.
River North
(312) 943-4059
M-F 7 A.M.-7 P.M., Sa 8 A.M.-4 P.M., Su 8 A.M.-2 P.M.

Connected to a salon next door, Cafe Josephine is a small neighborhood spot. The dining room is inviting with wicker chairs, marble table tops, and fresh-cut flowers. Josephine offers a full breakfast through lunch menu, and many of the large-portioned meals are under $5. The blended coffee is very good, and there seems to be an influx of regulars. This is a good place to stop if you're in the neighborhood.

Cafe Jumping Bean

1439 W. 18th St.
South Side
(312) 455-0019
M-Th 8 A.M.-10 P.M., F-Sa 8 A.M.-12 A.M. (closed Sundays)

$$

With brightly painted tables, live flamenco music, local art, and Spanish poetry readings, Cafe Jumping Bean is a terrific neighborhood alternative in the Hispanic area on the South Side. Most of the food items are Mexican; the chicken sandwich and pastel de tres leches cake are highly recommended. Also popular is the liquado, a drink similar to a milkshake in a variety of fruit flavors. Despite the iffy neighborhood, Cafe Jumping Bean attracts a crowd that varies in age and ethnicity, and it's a wonderful place for reading, talking, or simply people-watching. See coupon on page 119.

Cafe Luna
1908 W. 103rd St.
South Side/Beverly
(312) 239-8990
M-Th 6 A.M.-10 P.M., F-Sa 6 A.M.-11 P.M.

$$

Low prices are the main draw of this Beverly coffee shop. Their typical menu includes chili, gelato, baked goods, bottled juices, and sandwiches. You order from the counter and they bring it to you at your table. The seating is all tables and chairs, along with a children's corner offering books and crayons. You may read from a selection of books or local papers, and you won't pay too much for a good coffee. It's a neighborhood shop.

Café Mozart Espresso Bar 1/2
600 Davis St.
Evanston
(847) 492-8056
M-Th 7 A.M.-7 P.M., F-Sa 7 A.M.-11 P.M., Su 7 A.M.-8 P.M.

$$$

Vienna invades Evanston at the Café Mozart Espresso Bar. Although the light fare is somewhat typical, they offer a few low-fat alternatives and substantial lunch items. The coffee is tasty, and the cafe itself offers enough space to spread out. The soothing classical music makes reading easy. This cafe attracts a nice mix of young and old and offers more quiet than the nearby coffeehouses.

Cafe Selmarie   1/2

2327 W. Giddings Ave.
Northwest
(312) 989-5595
Su 7 A.M.-9 P.M., Tu-Sa 7 A.M.-10 P.M. (closed Mondays)

$$$$

Tucked into a brick courtyard off Lincoln Square, Cafe Selmarie quietly announces itself. Inside, a bright bakery case shows off its fresh, trademark desserts, while to the right a small peach-and-green dining area accommodates visitors. The vintage jazz plays softly, making reading or talking easy. The menu ranges from garlic bread to halibut to rich desserts, and the coffee drinks are all very good choices, particularly the flavorful and robust house blend. Although prices can get high (a minimum charge of

$4.25 during dinner hours) and a tip is necessary, this is a perfect place to satisfy a sweet tooth. See coupon on page 120.

Café 28   1/2
1800 W. Irving Park Rd.
North
(312) 528-2883
M-F 7 A.M.-7 P.M., Sa 8 A.M.-4 P.M.
    (Look for later hours Th, F, Sa)

*$$*1/2

This quiet corner shop near the Ravenswood el stop has a lot to offer a lunch visitor, with a menu of Cuban and Mexican specialties. Almost more of a restaurant than a coffeehouse, they offer enough light fare to take the coffee shop role. The coffee is good, the prices are reasonable, and the portions are generous. The table service is busy but efficient. Although not an artsy atmosphere, Café 28 has quite a few regulars and is quiet enough to read or talk.

Cafe Umbrella   1/2
4753 N. Lincoln Ave.
Northwest
(312) 275-7110
Daily 10 A.M.-10 P.M.

$$

Thick with secondhand smoke and a boisterous Italian crowd, this cafe offers an interesting alternative to Chicago's traditional coffee houses. The lattes are outstanding; no extras like syrup are offered, but none are needed. The music, television, and conversations make lone reading awkward, but it's a fun place to shoot the breeze.

Café Voltaire

3231 N. Clark St.
North
(312) 528-3136
M-Th 11:30 A.M.-11 P.M., F-Sa 11:30 A.M.-1 A.M.
   (closed Sundays)

$$$$

Voltaire's funky interior draws in visitors with art adorning the walls in vivid colors and textures. The vegetarian menu, high prices, and table service may frighten away some visitors, but it is worth a taste—the hummus and pates are delicious. The excruciatingly slow service leaves much to be desired, but the food is good, the coffee is fresh, and they offer music and performances in their Underground Performance Space.

Caffe Baci

231 S. LaSalle
Loop
(312) 629-1818
M-F 6:30 A.M.-6 P.M. (closed Saturdays and Sundays)

$$$$

Baci accommodates a busy lunch crowd daily but still manages elegant charm with dark wood decor, smooth black furniture, and three coveted, semiprivate window nooks. Most lunch items cost around $5 (average for the Loop), the coffee tastes fresh, and the desserts are plentiful. Try to avoid the noisy lunch crowd for a nice break.

Other location:
77 W. Wacker Dr., Loop, (312) 629-2224

Caffe Classico   1/2
400 S. LaSalle
Loop
(312) 987-0033
M-F 6 A.M.-5 P.M. (closed Saturdays and Sundays)

$$$

Classico is a bright shop with soft pink walls and lots of space to sit, frequented by those who work at the Board of Trade. Despite the plants and coffee sacks on the wall, this is still obviously a chain. Prices range from $1-2 for small coffee drinks, $3 for large drinks, $5 for salads and sandwiches, and pastries for around $1. The coffee drinks are occasionally served lukewarm, but most of the food, particularly the gelato, is tasty. If you're in the neighborhood, take a peek.

Other locations:
161 W. Madison, Loop (312) 782-0644
2 Prudential Plaza, Loop (312) 856-1400

Caffé Florian

1450 E. 57th St.
South
(312) 752-4100
Su-Th 11 A.M.-12 A.M., F-Sa 11 A.M.-1 A.M.

$$$

Based upon one of Venice's first coffeehouses, which opened in 1720 under the same name, Caffé Florian continues the original establishment's aim of providing a gathering place for the exchange of radical ideas and gossip. With tables and booths, African-American art decorating the peachy walls, and a largely collegiate crowd, Florian has a great atmosphere for discussion. The extensive menu ranges from gourmet to grease, and they offer a truly global selection of coffee beans and brewing methods. Although you will need to tip the wait staff, the prices are generally low.

Caffe Latté

3502 N. Harlem Ave.
Northwest
(312) 889-6807
Daily 5 P.M.-2 A.M. (hours may vary)

$$

Another one of Little Italy's adventures, Caffe Latté offers plenty of soccer memorabilia, hard liquor, beer, wine, and, of course, espresso. The language is mostly Italian, and the interior is dark, smoky, and limited to four tables and a pool table. The espresso is very good, not terribly strong, and the prices are low.

Caffé Pergolesi
3404 N. Halsted Ave.
North
(312) 472-8602
Su-Tu 9 A.M.-11:30 P.M., W-Th 10 A.M.-11:30 P.M.,
   F-Sa 9 A.M.-11:30 P.M. (hours may vary)

$$

First opened in 1967, the very popular Pergolesi was closed for a while. It has reopened its doors without losing its character. Spotty lighting and dark corners make it a perfect place for scribbling rhetoric in the midst of chess players, poets, readers, and chatters. The grungy interior and scattered tables and chairs echo the relaxed beatnik atmosphere. A sign outside reads "Life is too short to wear uncomfortable shoes or drink bad coffee. Come on in—we have good coffee." The food is excellent as well. And while you're there, take off those shoes.

Black as hell, strong as death, sweet as love.
—Turkish proverb

Caffe Trevi

2275 N. Lincoln
North
(312) 871-4310
M-Th 7 A.M.-11 P.M., F-Sa 7 A.M.-12 A.M., Su 8 A.M.-11 P.M.

$$

Local artists' colorful murals decorate the exposed brick walls of this alternative Lincoln Park hangout. Trevi offers plenty of games, periodicals ranging from the *New Yorker* to *National Geographic*, and conversation amid soothing contemporary music. The menu includes an outstanding vegetarian chili, hummus, basic pastries, and the white chocolate mousse cake with Oreos is worth a trip from anywhere. Count on the coffee being served fresh and warm.

Cappuccino Alfredo

 1/2

1509 W. Taylor Ave.
West
(312) 243-1177
M-F 9 A.M.-7 P.M.; Sa 7 A.M.-4:30 P.M. (closed Sundays)

$$

This Little Italy shop offers a nice light lunch and dinner menu full of authentic Italian pastas, pizzas, and sandwiches. Alfredo also offers a full line of espresso drinks; all are made authentically Italian and taste great. Don't miss the tiramisu. The window front brings in lots of sunlight, and every table has flowers in casual containers. If you're in the neighborhood, give it a try.

Capra's Coffee

2308 N. Clark St.
North
(312) 665-7182
M-F 6:30 A.M.-8 P.M., Sa 7 A.M.-8 P.M., Su 8 A.M.-7 P.M.

$$

Situated in a tiny storefront, Capra's doesn't have much space for character, but it is a good place to take out a cup in the morning. A few stools invite people-watching, the *Wall Street Journal* and the *Chicago Tribune* are available, and they offer some low-fat and vegetarian entrees. Although the foods don't always appear to be their freshest, the coffee is good, the service is quick, and the conversation is pleasant. See coupon on page 121.

Casa Java

2819 N. Southport Ave.
North
(312) 883-0238
M-Th 6:30 A.M.-10 P.M., F-Sa 7:30 A.M.-12 A.M.,
    Su 7:30 A.M.-10 P.M.

$$1/2

This Lakeview shop is a brilliant example of what a neighborhood coffeehouse should be. With brightly colored tables, chairs, cabinets, walls, and counter, Casa Java instantly attracts visitors. The barrista is extremely friendly to regulars and strangers alike. A large basket of big slippers waits downstairs, while in the upper loft you can find a book for exchange (take one book, leave one book). They offer basic pastries, cookies, desserts, and lunch fare, a long list of specialty lattes, including the banana cream, turtle sundae, raspberry truffle, and honey latte, as well as smoothies and iced drinks.

Coffee Chicago
3257 N. Broadway Ave.
North
(312) 244-0762
Hours vary by location

$$$

If you want to support a local chain, Coffee Chicago may be just right for you. With several north side locations, the shops have a uniform look and typically good coffee at comparatively low prices. The Broadway shop has particularly nice jazz playing on the sound system and a quiet atmosphere, although the service can be somewhat abrupt. The seating is all tables, and this is an ideal spot for reading the Sunday paper, people-watching, or chatting.

Other locations:
1561 N. Wells, North (312) 787-1211
2922 N. Clark, North (312) 327-3228
3323 N. Clark, North (312) 447-3323
5256 N. Broadway, Far North (312) 784-1305
5400 N. Clark, Far North (312) 907-8674

Corona's Coffee Shop

909 W. Irving Park Rd.
North
(312) 871-6989
Su-Th 7 A.M.-9 P.M., F 7 A.M.-9:30 P.M., Sa 9 A.M.-10 P.M.

$$

This small north side shop offers seating from a couch to counters to tables, but most of the visitors seem to be commuters. The atmosphere doesn't lend itself to long visits, but the coffee is fresh and tasty, the barrista is skilled, and the light fare is relatively inexpensive. With a television in the corner, this could be an interesting alternative for a Bulls game and some conversation.

---

*The morning cup of coffee has an exhilaration about it which the
cheering influence of the afternoon or evening cup of
tea cannot be expected to reproduce.*
—Oliver Wendell Holmes, *Over the Teacups* (1891)

Corby Coffee

2458 N. Lincoln Ave.
North
(312) 472-8535
M-Th 6 A.M.-10 P.M., F 6 A.M.-12 A.M., Sa 7 A.M.-12 A.M.,
    Su 7 A.M.-10 P.M.

$$

Corby offers little in terms of tangible decor, but take a deep sniff when you walk in the door and experience the aromatic atmosphere of the roasting coffee beans. The coffee itself is on the strong side, and the scones and pumpkin breads are very good. Although not an ideal place to read or talk, serious coffee drinkers will find a haven here.

Cream City Cafe

1 S. State St.
Carson Pirie Scott (Wabash entrance)
South Loop
(312) 641-7000
Hours vary

$$

If you don't mind eating in a department store, Cream City is ideal. Located within Carson's in a small area, it features a goodly amount of seating, a limited selection of coffee drinks and light fare, and quick service. This is a perfect pick-me-up for tired shoppers.

Damato's House of Coffee

1123 W. Grand Ave.
Loop
(312) 733-5488
M-F 7 A.M.-6 P.M., Sa 8 A.M.-4 P.M. (closed Sundays)

$$1/2

This small, lunch-intensive shop stands out in the industrial neighborhood west of the Loop. Although they offer inexpensive meals (most between $4 and $5), the coffee drinks cost more than most shops. However, take a peek (and a taste) of the ten varieties of mousse, tiramisu, and other desserts. The television may make reading difficult, but conversations flourish. See coupon on page 123.

Don's Coffee Club

1439 W. Jarvis Ave.
Far North
(312) 274-1228
Su-W 7 P.M.-1 A.M., F-Sa 7 P.M.-1 A.M. (closed Thursdays)

$$

Even if you weren't alive during the '40s and '50s, you can relive these decades at Don's Coffee Club in Rogers Park. With the thrift store decor of a college apartment and big band music playing endlessly, this smoky cafe attracts a young, friendly crowd. The limited seating is a blessing; you can meet a lot of people, including the nonchalant resident cat. The unpretentious, comfort-food menu consists of desserts and snacks, and don't expect an espresso here—only coffee in china cups and saucers. Bottomless coffees rarely go empty and the $2-$3 dessert portions are immense. Don also offers ballroom dancing outside on summer Sunday nights. Be sure to bring a friend along; although the neighborhood is a bit rough, this is cafe is one of best. See coupon on page 124.

Earwax Cafe

1564 N. Milwaukee Ave.
West
(312) 772-4019
M-Th 11 A.M.-12 A.M., F 11 A.M.-1 A.M., Sa 10 A.M.-1 A.M.,
    Su 10 A.M.-11 P.M.

$$$

Nose rings, loud music, and chatter abound in this Wicker Park cafe. The extensive menu features health-conscious, vegetarian entrees and the full range of coffees, although they tend to be weak. Earwax sells CDs and rents videos. The decor is wild and fun. Gentle readers, beware: the servers have taken the Ed Debevic's theme to a new level. However, the tasty food and alternative atmosphere are worth a trip.

Racine will go out of style like coffee.
—Marie de Rabutin-Chantal, Marquise de Sévigné

Emerald City Coffee Bar

3928 N. Sheridan Rd.
North
(312) 525-7847
M-F 5:30 A.M.-8 P.M., Sa 7 A.M.-8 P.M., Su 7 A.M.-7 P.M.

*$$*1/2

This small and cozy North Lakeview coffeehouse offers a comfortable couch, a handful of tables, bright sunlight from the large windows, and a piano and guitar for impromptu performances. Although the coffee is served extremely hot, it tastes fresh and is reasonably priced, as is the rest of the basic cafe menu. Owned by coffee-savvy Seattleites, Emerald City provides a relaxed neighborhood hangout with all the comforts of home. See coupon on page 125.

Emma G's

1309 E. 53rd St.
Hyde Park
(312) 684-2900
M-F 11 A.M.-11 P.M., Sa-Su 10:30 A.M.-5 P.M.

$$

This out-of-the-way shop presents itself as a vegetarian mecca in a meat-eating world. A number of the meatless dishes are good, and they range from Indian to Middle Eastern to European. They are also one of the few places in town to offer mushroom tea, which is proported to give your body a wonderful meta-physical reaction on your first sip. The yellow walls and colorful murals are fun, but overall Emma G's still has potential to fill with its somewhat grungy look and a few dishes not worthy of Mecca.

Ennui Cafe

1/2

6981 N. Sheridan Rd.
Far North
(312) 973-2233
Daily 7:30 A.M.-11 P.M.

$$

"Ennui" is French for a particular kind of boredom or weariness. This shop, eye-level with the sidewalk, offers the basic cafe fare at reasonable prices (most dishes are $2 or under), big picture windows that bring in lots of light, and lattes served in big heavy glass mugs. The plain white walls are sometimes bare and some-times filled with art, the seating can be cramped with only tables and chairs. If the conversation level is any indication, Ennui is frequented by regulars who swear by this unpretentious cafe to cure boredom.

Espresso Pacifico

10 E. Deleware Place
Near North
(312) 951-6455
M-Th 7 A.M.-6 P.M., F-Sa 7 A.M.-11 P.M., Su 8 A.M.-6 P.M.

$$$

This Gold Coast shop offers two floors of elegant decor, featuring works by local artists, as well as games and books. The somewhat higher price for the drinks, which are small, is offset by free refills. They offer basic light cafe fare. This is a quiet escape for a cup of coffee, but may not be worth going out of your way for a visit. If you are in the area, try it out.

Fonté Coffee Company 1/2
2504 N. Clark St.
North
(312) 528-9274
M-F 6 A.M.-8 P.M., Sa-Su 7 A.M.-8 P.M.

$$$

The Lincoln Park location of this small chain is a spacious pedestrian thoroughfare to the Lincoln Park Market. Decorated like a brown Starbucks, Fonté offers standard beverages along with various grilled panini sandwiches and other light fare. The service is quick and attentive, and they generate quite a bit of traffic. Customers seem to enjoy the busy atmosphere, and it doesn't hurt that the coffee, although usually served too hot to drink immediately, is outstanding.

Other location:
46 S. Clark St., Loop (312) 422-0142

Garson's Gourmet Coffee Café

1/2

5279 N. Elston Ave.
Northwest
(312) 286-4814
M-F 6 A.M.-7 P.M., Sa-Su 8 A.M.-7 P.M.

$$

This small Forest Glen shop is difficult to spot with its muted colors and unassuming storefront. The gingham curtains in the window and handmade craft decor suggest a displaced Wisconsin country kitchen. They offer the basic snacks for breakfast and dessert: muffins, scones, cheesecake, and cookies, along with a good selection of whole beans. The service is extremely friendly, and most of the clientele appear to be regulars. With a pervasive quiet cheer, this is a nice place for a talk or a book.

Gloria Jean's Coffee Beans

835 N. Michigan Ave.
Water Tower Place
(312) 944-7767
M-Th 10 A.M.-7 P.M., F 9:30 A.M.-8 P.M., Sa 9 A.M.-7 P.M.,
  Su 11 A.M.-6 P.M.

*$$*1/2

If you are looking for a bag of beans, bottles of syrup, some mugs, a tea collection, or any other coffee merchandise, Gloria

Jean's is the place to shop. You can also stop for a takeout cup and treats to eat on your way to work. Most of the downtown locations don't have much seating space. Instead, they concentrate on premiere gourmet goodies to give as gifts or to enjoy yourself. See coupons on pages 126–127.

Other locations:
Merchandise Mart, North Loop (312) 527-4929
Palmer House, Loop (312) 606-0688
101 N. Wacker Dr., Loop (312) 368-8559
111 W. Jackson St., Loop (312) 461-9305
131 W. Madison Ave., Loop (312) 630-1970
135 S. LaSalle, Loop (312) 578-9225
222 S. Riverside Plaza, West (312) 443-1412

Godiva Chocolatier

835 N. Michigan Ave.
Water Tower Place
Near North
(312) 280-1133
M-F 10 A.M.-9 P.M., Sa 9:30 A.M.-9 P.M., Su 11 A.M.-6 P.M.

$$

With standard glass walls, marbled peach tile, and a raspberry mousse ceiling, Godiva in Water Tower will attract your sweet tooth. Although not an ideal place to pass the time, if a coffee or chocolate craving arises while you're shopping, this is the perfect place to stop. The hazelnut coffee is somewhat strong, and the chocolate and desserts are legendary. See coupon on page 128.

Gourmand Coffeehouse

728 S. Dearborn
Loop
(312) 427-2610
M-Th 7 A.M.-11 P.M., F 7 A.M.-12 A.M., Sa 8 A.M.-12 A.M.,
  Su 8 A.M.-11 P.M.

$$$

Gourmand is an eclectic haven for atmosphere junkies roaming
for something other than a major chain south of the Loop. With
warm rose walls, a couch in the corner, and jazz and acoustic
music on weekends, Gourmand is a nice addition to the historic
Printer's Row area. The food is usually fresh, they offer low-fat
alternatives, and they serve an interesting assortment of lesser-
known beer. The service can be slow and inefficient at times, but
Gourmand will please anyone looking for a brief escape. See
coupon on page 129.

Gourmet Cup Coffee

50 W. Adams St.
Loop
(312) 701-0222
M-F 6 A.M.-6 P.M. (closed Saturdays and Sundays)

$$

Similar to Starbucks, Gourmet Cup offers much the same as its
competitor. However, the service is usually good, and the coffee

is nothing to sneeze at. At last visit, they offered a 12 oz. latte for $1.99, a good price in the heart of the Loop. For an inexpensive alternative without sacrificing quality, Gourmet Cup is worth a takeout order.

Other locations
203 N. Wabash, Loop (312) 629-5336
2531 N. Clark St., North (312) 327-3634
2591 N. Broadway, North (312) 327-6645

Great Lakes Coffee and Tea, Ltd.

1517 W. Foster Ave.
Far North
506-1500
M-Th 7 A.M.-7 P.M., F 7 A.M.-11 P.M., Sa 9 A.M.-11 P.M.,
    Su 9 A.M.-7 P.M.

$$

This small, inviting Andersonville coffeehouse is for book lovers as well as coffee lovers, with plenty of hardcover and paperback books for sale ranging from classics to trash. They also offer quite a few coffees and teas for sale, and provide the standard cafe fare of muffins, scones, bagels, soups, and desserts. Most drinks are between $1 and $2.50, and the foods don't cost much more. Great Lakes is a fine neighborhood hangout where you can read, talk, or relax-try the patio on summer afternoons.

Coffee induces wit.
—Gustave Flaubert

Grind & Brew Coffeehouse

1920 W. Irving Park Rd.
North
(312) 348-7592
M 6 A.M.-8 P.M., Tu-F 6 A.M.-11 P.M., Sa 5 A.M.-11 P.M.,
    Su 9 A.M.-4 P.M.

$$

You can't miss this Lakeview coffeehouse with its bright orange storefront. Once inside, you find a spacious, down-to-earth shop with borrowed furniture, art, books, magazines, lamps, and a big counter. The menu is somewhat limited, but the prices are low, the coffee is brewed strong, and the hot chocolate is wonderful—it's creamy, chocolatey, and served with whipped cream and a big marshmallow. They offer live music, poetry readings, toys for kids and for adults (coming soon—two computers connected to the Internet). Grind & Brew is a fun neighborhood hangout with something for everyone. See coupon on page 130.

Halsted Street Digital Audio Café

3641 N. Halsted St.
North
(312) 325-CAFE
M-Th 10 A.M.-2 A.M., F 10 A.M.-4 A.M., Sa 10 A.M.-5 A.M.,
    Su 10 A.M.-12 A.M.

$$

You might easily miss the Halsted Street Digital Audio Café, located in a refurbished garage with only a small sign and a few lights to announce its presence. But once inside under a cavernous ceiling, this cafe is surprisingly warm, inviting, and comfortable. They offer a variety of quality foods from pizza, desserts, pastries, and sandwiches. They also offer a full range of coffee drinks, including a "booster" (espresso brewed with a packet of sugar). Used CDs for sale line the walls; the selection is limited—you probably won't find anything particular or rare—but at prices from $4-$9, the bins are worth a look. See coupon on page 131.

Hardboiled

7101 N. Ridge Ave.
Far North
Su-Th 7 A.M.-10 P.M., F-Sa 7 A.M.-12 P.M.

$1/2

This West Rogers Park establishment offers a wonderful Chinese decor with marble octagon tables, bamboo birdcages, paper lanterns, and a large stone fountain in the front. The menu is sparse; they offer muffins and bagels along with two kinds of soup and a noodle dish. They serve what they do have in lovely Chinese cups (careful, without handles they get hot) and on real plates. The classical music and natural sunlight add a nice backdrop to a book or a conversation.

Hardcastle's Coffee & Tea Emporium

500 W. Madison Ave.
West
648-0070
M-F 5:30 A.M.-12:30 A.M., Sa-Su 9 A.M.-11:30 P.M.

$1/2

Located in Union Station, Hardcastle's offers a full selection of teas and coffees within a newsstand and snack shop. The service is friendly and cheerful, the coffee is more reasonably priced than most places, and it tastes good. Enviromentalists beware: drinks are served in styrofoam cups. But otherwise, this is a good stop to and from the train. See coupon on page 132.

Higher Ground

1999 S. Campus Dr.
Northwestern University Norris Center
Evanston
(847) 491-2300
M-Th 8 A.M.-12 A.M., F-Sa 8 A.M.-2 A.M., Su 10 A.M.-12 A.M.

$$

Located within the Norris Center on the Northwestern University campus, Higher Ground consists of an espresso cart next to a redecorated section of the student union. Large, comfortable chairs and couches are grouped together, while funky lamps and tables complete the tacky vintage decor. As expected, the crowd is mostly academic, and the place fills up after the dinner hours. Although the selection is limited, the coffee is usually fresh, the hot chocolate is thick, and the prices are low. Look for the daily specials, live music on the nearby stage, and an outstanding view of the lake.

Higher Ground

2022 W. Roscoe Ave.
Northwest
(312) 868-0075
M-Th 7 A.M.-10 P.M., F 7 A.M.-12 A.M., Sa 8 A.M.-12 A.M.,
    Su 9 A.M.-10 P.M.

$$

With a huge picture window full of plants, dried flowers, and antique candle holders, Higher Ground offers a welcome hideaway for a book or a discussion. Although the menu is limited, the homemade muffins are some of the best, and entire selection of food is fresh and served in generous portions. You can slouch on the sofas with a book or newspaper from their collection or sit up at the counter in the back. Altogether, it is a laid-back experience. See coupon on page 134.

Coffee is a fleeting moment and a fragrance.
—Claudia Roden

Intelligentsia

1/2

3123 N. Broadway Ave.
North
(312) 348-8058
Winter hours: M-F 6 A.M.-10 P.M., Sa-Su 7 A.M.-11 P.M.
Summer hours: call

$$

Intelligentsia is more than an elegant cafe—it's a coffee roaster, tea blender, and educational center all in one. With approximately thirty blends of coffee and twenty blends of tea available, you'll be sure to find variety and freshness (no coffee is sold more than seven days after they roast it in the store). If you buy a coffee drink there, they serve it in glass cups. On takeout orders, the lid comes on the side so you can see the coffee masterpiece you are getting. Purchasing an espresso machine there will result in extensive help learning how to use it. The store itself is spacious with subdued wood, lime green decor, and plenty of seats for a chat or a read. This is a must-visit for anyone serious about coffee. See coupon on page 135.

Interactive Bean

1137 W. Belmont Ave.
North
(312) 528-2996
M-Th 6:30 A.M.-11 P.M., F 6:30 A.M.-12 P.M.,
    Sa 7:30 A.M.-12 A.M., Su 7:30 A.M.-6 P.M.

$$

Situated on a lonely stretch of Belmont, Interactive Bean is well worth the out-of-the-way location for the outstanding coffee alone. This spacious cafe has Macintosh computers in various settings throughout: private nooks, by a comfortable couch, and in the windows. Rental is $9.60/hour with full Internet access, computer games, and whatnot. Scanning, printing, and instruction are also available. The walls have a vibrant paint job, and books, games, and computer magazines are available. The food offerings are sparse, but they plan to expand their menu to include desserts, soups, and other light fare. See coupon on page 136.

Island Java

947 W. Addison
North
(312) 525-0299
M-F 6 A.M.-9 P.M., Sa 7 A.M.-9 P.M., Su 8 A.M.-9 P.M.

$$$

One of Wrigleyville's newest cafes, Island Java is a small corner store directly under the el stop at Addison. This is a perfect stop for commuters who want to grab a cup before getting on the train. Try the Island bar, a unique dessert concoction with chocolate chips and macadamia nuts while you sample the selection of magazines and games. There is occasional live music and a bonus for Cubs fans: they sell a selection of cigars (for smoking at the ballpark, not in the shop). See coupon on page 137.

Jacobs Bros. Java   ☕☕☕1/2
53 W. Jackson St.
Loop
(312) 922-5282
M-F 6 A.M.-6 P.M.

$$

Next door to Jacobs Bros. Bagels, a Chicago institution, lies the sister shop, Java. Located in the historic Monadnock Building, the interior reflects the gorgeous architecture and vintage floor tiles. Although they have some space for sitting and reading, the commuter takeout counter is the center of activity. The bagels are fresh from next door, and the coffee is fresh, as well. You can get a large coffee and a bagel for $2—a bargain in the Loop. Java offers the basics, and they do it well.

Jamoch's Caffe Ltd.   ☕☕☕1/2
1066 W. Taylor Ave.
(312) 226-7666
West
M-F 7 A.M.-9 P.M., Sa 9 A.M.-6 P.M. (closed Sundays)

$$$

At first glance, Jamoch's appears to be a classic coffeehouse with steamed-up front windows, a few books scattered on the sills, peeling letters, and a few houseplants. However, inside you'll find an inexpensive art deco look with black and white floor tile, marbled tables, and bright paint. The service is very friendly and unpretentious. You can expect a large student turnout, especially during lunch. They offer a nice breakfast, enough quiet to read, enough noise to talk, and a pretty good cup of joe.

Java Centrale

2204 N. Clark St.
North
(312) 472-5858
M-Th 6:30 A.M.-10 P.M., F-Sa 6:30 A.M.-11 P.M.,
　Su 7 A.M.-10 P.M.

$$

Offering fine gourmet coffees, Java Centrale has a menu a step above your average chain. Various salads, soups, and light fare are also available, and the breakfast fare is baked fresh every day. Home brewers will like the huge selection of whole bean coffees from around the world. They offer more sandwiches than most, which makes this a good lunch and dinner alternative, but you won't quite escape the chain feeling.

Java Express

10701 S. Hale St.
South Side
233-8557
M-F 6 A.M.-6 P.M., Sa 7 A.M.-4 P.M., Su 8 A.M.-2 P.M.

$$

This somewhat smoky shop offers a nice lunch menu of two soups daily and a variety of sandwiches. One of the older coffee-houses in Beverly, the crowd is mostly local and very friendly. They bake most of their offerings, including wonderfully sweet and heavy raisin scones, and their coffee is typically fresh. A sign near the door notes the Metra train times for the station a half block away, and the service is refreshingly cheerful. Worth a visit while in historic Beverly. See coupon on page 138.

Java Joans
119 N. Marion Ave.
Oak Park
(708) 524-5282
M-F 7:30 A.M.-6:30 P.M., Sa 6:30 A.M.-5 P.M., Su 10 A.M.-5 P.M.

$$$

Situated in a revamped street mall in downtown Oak Park, Java Joan's offers a nice bright stop while in town. The light blue walls, comfortably worn fixtures, and plenty of counter seating give this shop a 1950s diner feel, while the large windows allow lots of sunlight and people-watching. The coffee is fresh and flavorful, and although the menu is not extensive, the hot Ghiradelli chocolate and steamed Thai coffee show an emphasis on quality. A good place to stop if you're shopping in Oak Park.

Java Thai

1/2

4272 W. Irving Park Rd.
Northwest
(312) 545-6200
M-Th 8 A.M.-10 P.M., F-Sa 8 A.M.-11 P.M., Su 8 A.M.-4 P.M.

$$$

Tucked in the basement corner of an Old Irving Park courtyard apartment building, Java Thai is a treasured find. With exposed brick walls, lots of mellow wood, sturdy tables, and nifty lamps, they offer a cozy atmosphere in an unexpected setting. Servings are fresh, large, and tasty, and they feature Thai dishes as an alternative to regular cafe fare. This is worth a detour for an afternoon of conversation or contemplation, reading or writing.

Jazzy Cafe

1155 W. Diversey Pkwy.
North
(312) 296-2169
M-F 7:30 A.M.-8:30 P.M., Sa 9 A.M.-8 P.M., Su 9 A.M.-3 P.M.

$$

One of the blue-collar cafes in the city, Jazzy is more of a sandwich shop than a coffeehouse. However, they offer basic coffee and espresso drinks along with their sandwiches for breakfast, lunch, and dinner. The service is friendly and casual, and the food is fresh and well made. Coffee aficionados may be disappointed.

J. K. Sweets

716-1/2 Clark St.
Evanston
(847) 864-3073
Daily 7:30 A.M.-midnight

*$$*1/2

With all of the wonderful coffee shops in Evanston, J. K. Sweets may find itself down a ways on your list. Although it had a gray marbled makeover a few years ago, the overall quality could be higher. The muffins are good, and they bake most of their foods, but the coffee and desserts are sometimes stale. The service is often good, despite a confusing traffic pattern. J. K.'s is worth a stop for ice cream, yogurt, or a morning muffin, but you'll find better coffee at other Evanston coffeehouses.

Joe Mocha

5440 N. Sheridan Rd.
Far North
(312) 275-1224
Daily 6:30 A.M.-5 P.M.

$$

Squeezed into a hidden nook beside a motel on Sheridan Road, Joe Mocha is one of Chicago's odder coffee shops. The decor is somewhat generic. There are reading materials, including *Glamour* and *Town and Country.* Few of the servers speak English. But the hazelnut coffee is quite good, they offer basic cafe pastries, and they have numerous fresh-squeezed juices, including ginger and carrot. Although not ideal as a hangout, this is worth a stop for the unusual juice and the low price.

Kafein
1621 Chicago Ave.
Evanston
(847) 491-1621
Su-Th 9 A.M.-2 A.M., F-Sa 11 A.M.-4 A.M.

$$$

Most likely the only shop in the Chicago area with a fresco of Michelangelo's God handing Adam a cup of joe at the moment of creation, Kafein is a wild alternative to Evanston's more conservative establishments. With dusty Victorian couches and dim lighting, Kafein attracts a young crowd, but you need not feel angst to feel at home with the offering of books, games, live music, and readings. A large menu boasts several soups and salads, pastries, and desserts. The coffee alone is worth the trip—try the caffeine-charged Zombie. Although prices loom high, the portions are large and filling. Leave a tip for the table service. See coupon on page 139.

Kokomo Caffe
905 W. Belmont Ave.
North
(312) 404-2233
Su-Th 8 A.M.-10 P.M., F-Sa 8 A.M.-1 A.M.

$$1/2

Decorated with posters and an interesting plant sculpture, Kokomo offers a no-frills relaxed atmosphere for everyone. With several counters and lots of tables there's plenty of room, and readers will enjoy the nooks equipped with lamps. The service is extremely friendly and efficient, the menu offers everything from egg dishes to pastas to ice cream, and the coffee is very good. They have a front counter that operates on the honor system for commuters. Although a tip is obligatory, prices are reasonable. Weekends bring crowds and plenty of secondary smoke.

Kopi, A Traveler's Cafe

5317 N. Clark St.
Far North
(312) 989-5674
M-Th 8 A.M.-11 P.M., F 8 A.M.-12 A.M., Sa 9 A.M.-12 A.M.,
    Su 10 A.M.-11 P.M.

$$$1/2

Conceptually, the Andersonville cafe is promising: devoted to travel, this shop provides helpful travel advisors and a network of wanderlusters. In reality, however, it doesn't quite work. The travel books are for sale only and are in a small bookshelf cramped too close to nearby tables for browsing. The table service tends to be slow and unresponsive. One the plus side, the food selection is global and tasty, and the coffee is very good. A platform up front, strewn with pillows, offers cozy comfort, with house slippers for shoeless platform sitters (it's the rule). Despite some minor kinks, Kopi has a lot to offer. See coupon on page 140.

Krystyna's Cafe
8 E. Jackson St.
Loop
(312) 922-9225
Daily 7:30 A.M.-6 P.M.

$1/2

Walk into Krystyna's and you'll think you've entered a Renoir painting. The interior is fashioned as an outdoor garden with bright colors, pastels, and table umbrellas. The menu is thoroughly European, with a wide selection of pizzas, muffins, sandwiches, and coffee drinks. The coffee is a bit weak, but the Plumkunchen muffin is fantastic and most of the fare is fresh. The price is also worth the trip: an advertised special was $1.55 for a coffee and muffin. An idyllic alternative to busy downtown lunch spots.

La Madeleine
2815 N. Broadway Ave.
North
(312) 477-2111
Su-Th 7 A.M.-10 P.M., F-Sa 7 A.M.-11 P.M.

$$$$

This French bakery chain's cafeteria-style service combined with counter service may result in minor confusion since some items can be ordered via the cafeteria line while others require a special request. Although the prices for certain food items is high, it's quite fresh and tasty, and the coffees are bottomless. The warm hearths and provincial bistro decor give La Madeleine a comfortable, soothing atmosphere.

La Piazza
3845 N. Broadway Ave.
North
(312) 868-0998
M, W-Su 8 A.M.-11 P.M. (closed Tuesdays)

$$$

If you're looking for a place with a comfortable atmosphere, friendly service, a varied selection, and outstanding coffee, you have found it in La Piazza. This spacious north side cafe offers enough space for smokers and nonsmokers, games and books for the bored, and comfortable couches for the weary. Offering several blends daily, the coffee is fresh and expertly brewed, and a new espresso machine makes excellent lattes and cappuccinos. A unique offering is the green apple cider (freshly brewed from granny smith apples). La Piazza is a definite find. See coupon on page 141.

Liberty Coffee & Teas

401 S. LaSalle Ave.
Loop
(312) 786-5282
M-F 6 A.M.-6 P.M. (closed Saturdays and Sundays)

*$$*1/2

Occupying the corner of a cafeteria-style deli, Liberty attempts atmosphere with festive decor around their counter—and they pull it off to some degree. The casual, friendly service is also a nice draw. They offer the basic coffee drinks, muffins, scones, and pastries (sometimes half off for day-old items). They have tables, Liberty's best offer is a good cup of coffee for the commuter on the go.

Little Miss Muffin

721 W. Grand Ave.
West
(312) 455-6328
hours

$$$

Oh wow—if you thought you've had some good muffins in your life, you need to try Little Miss Muffin to see what you've been missing. As suppliers to many of Chicago's coffee shops, you may have tried some of their muffins, but you can't beat the fresh warmth and huge selection on site at their River West bakery. In contrast to the industrial neighborhood, the cafe has a cheerful gourmet decor, and the service is extremely nice. Don't miss the lemon drop cookies; they are the best in the city.

Logan Beach

2537 N. Kedzie Blvd.
Northwest
(312) 862-4277
Su-Th 7 A.M.-12 A.M., F-Sa 8:30 A.M.-12 A.M.

$$1/2

At first glance, Logan Beach strongly resembles a hole in the wall, but once inside, you'll find a comfortable home. The mostly homemade menu covers breakfast through dessert, and prices are lower than most places. The crowd ranges from twentysomethings to older babyboomers, and they all seem to know each other. They sell a selection of used books, a grand piano waits to be played, and your cappuccino may arrive in a mug painted with a puppy in a Santa Claus hat. (Mom, can I have some more?)

Lunar Cabaret and Full Moon Café

2827 N. Lincoln Ave.
North
(312) 327-6666
Tu-F 5 P.M.-1:30 A.M., Sa 11 A.M.-2 A.M., Su 11 A.M.-12 A.M.
   (closed Mondays)

$$$

With an unassuming, peeling blue storefront, Lunar Cafe seems a little down at the heels. Inside, however, you'll find an enjoyable spot. Featuring spoken-word performances, live music, and readings, they offer consistently entertaining shows for a low cover. The coffee is good, and the menu features some tasty light fare, including a feta and pine nut sandwich, spinach lasagna, and tempeh burgers. Drinks include the usual suspects along with lemonade, cream sodas, and floats. You may bring your own wine for a $2 corkage fee. Call for showtimes.

Lutz Continental Cafe and Pastry Shop 1/2

2458 W. Montrose Ave.
Far North
(312) 478-7785
Tu-Su 7 A.M.-10 P.M. (closed Mondays)

$$$

Connected to a German bakery, Lutz's offers a full range of light to large gourmet foods for somewhat reasonable prices. The European atmosphere is complete with Vienna coffee served by the pot on a silver tray with sugar, cream, and whipped cream on the side. The service is professional, swift, and extremely friendly, and they specialize in fresh, delicious desserts. Although prices can get higher than most, Lutz is a unique place to stop for some sweets.

Mad Bar & Cafe

1640 W. Damen Ave.

West

(312) 227-2277

Su-F 7 A.M.-2 A.M., Sa 8 A.M.-3 A.M. (Brunch served Su 10 A.M.-
3 P.M.)

$$$1/2

After dark, Mad Bar turns into a nightspot with three bars, a
stage, and pool table, but during the day it makes quite a nice
cafe. The strawberry-and-rust walls, large picture windows, and
tinny 1920s jazz make this a cheerful Sunday brunch stop. The
lattes and coffees are very good, and the brunch menu in partic-
ular is tasty and costs less than most other brunch stops. If you're
hungry for a meal and conversation, this is a good choice.

Mama Java's Cafe

705 Main St.

Evanston

(847) 733-1390

M-Sa 7 A.M.-11 P.M., Su 8 A.M.-10 P.M.

$$$1/2

Mama Java's offers people-watching and camaraderie in a com-
munity hangout. Despite the low light and noisy clientele, this

cafe is good for reading. The coffee is outstanding, if pricey at over $3 for a "huge" flavored latte. They also offer "baby" sizes and whites—a hot non-coffee drink. The food is fresh and includes things like ice cream and cold cereal, worth the extra price. They feature live music on Thursday through Saturday nights with cover charges ranging from $0-$5, art from local artists, and enough space to spread out and relax.

Mama's Paradise Cafe

1646 N. Damen Ave.
West
(312) 772-6770
M-Th 8 A.M.-10 P.M.; F-Sa 8 A.M.-11 P.M. (closed Sundays)

$$

Finding the bright orange storefront in Wicker Park is more difficult than it seems, but Mama's Paradise Cafe is worth the search. The interior has an intense paint job with vines climbing the walls, Christmas lights coiled around the pipes, and light jazz and blues playing on the sound system. A full-service restaurant as well, they have a counter for the regulars to shoot the breeze, and space for smokers and nonsmokers alike. The service is friendly and quick, the prices are low, and the food and coffee come fresh. Don't miss it.

Coffee in England is just toasted milk.
—Christopher Fry, *New York Post*, November 29, 1962

Medici

1327 E. 57th St.
South
(312) 667-7394
M-F 7 A.M.-12:30 A.M., Sa 9 A.M.-1 A.M., Su 9 A.M.-12:30 A.M.

$$$

One of Chicago's original coffeehouses, Medici is now a full-service restaurant. According to the owner and *Chicago* magazine, employees at the Medici invented eggs espresso. This casual stop in Hyde Park is usually full of University of Chicago students studying amid the noise. Bright and social, you can get a strong, college-style coffee for $1 and their legendary pizza for a little more.

Metro Espresso

322 S. Michigan Ave.
Loop

$1/2

The service is the only redeeming quality of Metro Espresso; they are friendly, relaxed, and fast. The storefront lacks any interesting atmosphere, the coffee is not necessarily fresh, and the limited seating is uncomfortable and awkward. The coffee itself is not worth a trip unless you're short on cash—they have lower prices than most Loop shops.

Michael's Gourmet Coffee

7714 W. Belmont Ave.
Northwest
(312) 625-6020
Daily 7 A.M.-12 A.M.

$

Michael's is a small, clean, and sparse storefront that specializes in the basics. Other than a few packaged snacks, they offer no food—only espresso. A latte costs a mere $1.50, and the few seats usually hold some Italian-speaking locals. The coffee is very fresh and flavorful and is sold by the pound either ground or whole beans.

Mozart Cafe

3727 N. Southport Ave.
North
(312) 348-1253
M-Th 11 A.M.-9:30 P.M., F 11 A.M.-12 P.M., Sa 9 A.M.-12 P.M.,
    Su 9 A.M.-9:30 P.M.

$$$$

The Mozart Cafe interior is a little surprising: huge murals of Mozart adorn the walls and large cherubs hang from the ceiling, while a neon Mozart buzzes quietly in the window. However, the cafe is nicely laid out with all tables. The menu contains a wide variety of pastas and appetizers, as well as coffee drinks. They have a $5 minimum, so the bill can get high. However, the food is fresh and tasty. A wonderful, albeit expensive stop after a good film at the Music Box. See coupon on page 142.

Nervous Center

4612 N. Lincoln Ave.
Northwest
(312) 728-5010
Tu-F 5 P.M.-2 A.M., Sa 5 P.M.-3:30 A.M., Su 10 A.M.-2 A.M.
  (closed Mondays)

$

First-time visitors to this Lincoln Square coffee shop will probably do a double take. They only have coffee, bagels, and cookies? Is that really a reggae version of "My Way"? Once you get used to coffee—they offer only coffee—you will like the dark atmosphere, the truly alternative music, and eclectic visitors. Check out the working 1907 coffee roaster in the back and the terrific thrift clothing for sale.

No Exit Cafe

6970 N. Glenwood Ave.
Far North
(312) 743-3355
M-Th 4 P.M.-12 A.M., F 1 P.M.-1 A.M., Sa 12 P.M.-1 A.M.,
  Su 11 A.M.-12 A.M.

$$$

Opened in 1958, No Exit is one of the oldest coffeehouses in the country; in Chicago, it is one of the most authentic. With art and objects scattered haphazardly and old furniture the rule, you'll find enough light to read, enough space to talk, and a generous menu from which to choose baked goods, soups, sandwiches, and salads. Especially enchanting is the daily metamorphosis: weekend mornings bring a bright brunch atmosphere, while by night No Exit becomes a dark, comfortable cabaret. See coupon on page 143.

Opera Cafe

1458 Sherman Ave.
Evanston
(847) 332-2742
Su, Tu-Th 11:30 A.M.-10:30 P.M., F-Sa 11:30 A.M.-11:30 P.M.
   (closed Mondays)

$$$$

The Opera Cafe offers an elegant, refined alternative to Evanston's many student hangouts. Featuring live opera Tuesday through Saturday, they provide a stage for Northwestern students and other singers to belt out pieces from selected operas. The desserts, Italian pastas, salads, and sandwiches are good, and the coffees are wonderful, although the service can be inconsistent. If you are looking for stimulating entertainment in an elegant setting, this is the place to go. See coupon on page 144.

Panini Panini

6764 N. Sheridan Rd.
Far North
(312) 761-7775
Daily 8 A.M.-12 A.M.

$$$

This quaint, family-managed European coffeehouse nestles in a quiet corner in Rogers Park. The menu consists of simple, light meals, terrific coffee, and usually fresh pastries. Although the seating can be cramped and the lighting dim, this is a fine place for a chess game, talking, or reading. A favorite among many Rogers Park residents for a soothing afternoon or evening.

Perk: A Drink House

3322 N. Halsted Ave.
North
(312) 549-9900
M-W 4 P.M.-1 A.M., Th-Su 12 P.M.-1 A.M.

$$$$

Don't call Perk a coffeehouse—as the name suggests, this is a serious place for drinks, with marbled walls, a menu on rolls of craft paper, and a huge stone counter. The large menu consists mainly of specially concocted drinks, categorized as coffees, espressos, cappuccinos, lattes, shakes, and steamed milks. They offer a rotating menu of desserts, including an outstanding flourless white chocolate mousse cake. With house music and dim lighting, this is an obvious alternative to a bar, so leave your book at home. The servers are friendly and extremely knowledgeable, and despite the serious menu, Perk is a lot of fun.

Rok Coffee Emporium

5067 N. Lincoln Ave.
Far North
(312) 334-3898
M-Th 12 P.M.-12 A.M., F-Sa 12 P.M.-1 A.M., Su 12 P.M.-11 P.M.

$$$$

Rok lies like an oasis in the midst of crowded storefronts. Set back from the street by a parking lot, small white lights announce its presence. The spacious interior has tables with red and white tablecloths, a large central counter, and scattered paintings and drawings on the walls. The menu is mostly drinks and desserts, although they have a few interesting sandwiches including Swiss cheese and apple, as well as banana and peanut butter. They sell a selection of brewing equipment in a corner and offer live jazz on occasional weekends. The black light in the bathroom is somewhat unsettling, but overall, Rok is a nice surprise.

Among the numerous luxuries of the table . . . coffee may be considered as one of the most valuable.
—Benjamin Thompson

Roscoe's Coffeehouse

3354 N. Halsted Ave.

North

(312) 281-3355

Daily 12 P.M.-12 A.M. (generally open later on weekends)

$$$$

With memorabilia, signs, art, and statuettes filling the many shelves, Roscoe's offers a cluttered barlike atmosphere for coffee lovers. Loud house music and dim lighting make reading difficult, while the crowd seems to be regulars deep in conversation. They offer a full menu of appetizers, salads, soups, hot and cold sandwiches, and desserts, as well as basic coffee drinks. The servings are generous and popular, while the coffee is average. The connected bar offers live music, the coffeehouse being an alternative to the scene next door.

Saint Germain Bakery

1210 N. State St.

Near North

(312) 266-9900

Daily 8 A.M.-10 P.M.

$$$$

Although the menu is somewhat sparse, the atmosphere of this European-style bakery is quite inviting. Weekend mornings draw a large Gold Coast crowd, but the tables in the sunny rooms at the front are excellent for reading the morning paper. The coffee drinks are basic (no syrups are offered), and the final bill grows quickly, but St. Germain is a habit worth starting for the unusual and very fresh breads and pastries.

Savories

1700 N. Wells
North
(312) 951-7638
Daily 6:30 A.M.-7 P.M.

$$$

Incredibly cozy and casual, Savories offers excellent coffee and foods, with the added touch of unusual merchandise (stuffed animals, t-shirts, lava lamps). Extensive reading materials drift among the couches, plants, and other comforts as 93 WXRT plays softly over the speakers. Chat with a regular or one of the handful of celebrities that frequent this nine-year-old cafe, or just snuggle up with a good book. Don't forget to try the outstanding desserts.

Scenes Coffee House and Dramatist Bookstore

3168 N. Clark St.
North
(312) 525-1007
Su-Th 10:30 A.M.-11 P.M., F-Sa 10:30 A.M.-2:30 A.M.

$$$

The dark clothes and emoting voices are the first clues that the crowd at Scenes is a little different. This cafe sells their reading material—a wide offering of scripts, fiction, and anthologies (please buy before you sit). Ten tables are squeezed in among the shelves, yet there never seems to be congestion between browsers and drinkers. They allow smoking, which gets somewhat dispersed by the ceiling fan, and the seats by the windows are a bit chilly in cold weather. Because of the limited seating, staying long hours is discouraged, and you may be asked to share your table. However, the coffee drinks are wonderful and the foods are filling. Don't forget to tip your server. See coupon on page 145.

Seattle's Best Coffee
42 E. Chicago Ave.
Near North
(312) 337-0885
M-Th 6 A.M.-10 P.M., F 6 P.M.-11 P.M., Sa 7 A.M.-11 P.M.,
    Su 8 A.M.-9 P.M.

$$$

Along with another location on Wells Street, this new chain adds some nice touches for customers: real cups and plates for eating in, return visit cards, comfortable seating, and free samples of their regular blends. The staff is well trained and strives to make the perfect cup of coffee for every visitor, and they usually succeed. Although the light wood floors and tables, large stock posters, and muted lights make a pretty store, you may feel like you are sitting in a Gap. But this cafe has excellent coffee.

Other location:
701 N. Wells St., River North (312) 649-9452

Some Things Brewing 1/2
906 S. Oak Park Ave.
Oak Park
(708) 445-0010
M-Th 6 A.M.-9 P.M., F 6 A.M.-10 P.M., Sa 7 A.M.-10 P.M.,
    Su 8 A.M.-9 P.M.

$$$

Some Things Brewing offers a clean and comfortable if somewhat uninteresting neighborhood shop. They offer games and books, but the bland, weak coffee and clumsy takeout setup detracts from an enjoyable visit. Their basic cafe menu has a goodly array of breads, local free papers are available, and the service is attentive. This is a decent place to talk or read, but you can find better coffee elsewhere.

Starbucks

With over fifty outlets in Chicago and the suburbs, the green-and-black storefronts of Starbucks are becoming a familiar sight. Although many of the locations, particularly in the Loop, have limited seating, you are guaranteed some of the best coffee in the city at any of their outlets. And a visit to the world's largest Starbucks at 932 N. Rush is a must. Call individual locations for hours.

These are the Chicago, Evanston, and Oak Park locations as of January 1, 1996:

Barnes & Noble, 1701 Sherman Ave., Evanston (847) 328-0883
Barnes & Noble, 659 W. Diversey, North (312) 871-9004
Merchandise Mart, Loop (312) 661-0443
University of Chicago Bookstore, South Side (312) 702-8729
10 S. Riverside Plaza, Loop (312) 441-1919
35 E. Wacker Dr., Loop (312) 541-5317
35 W. Wacker Dr., Loop (312) 553-0244
39 W. Division St., Near North (312) 951-6992
70 W. Madison Ave., Loop (312) 357-0927
100 S. Wacker Dr., Loop (312) 759-5559
105 W. Adams, Loop (312) 855-0099
111 W. Washington Ave, Loop (312) 372-1331
150 N. Wacker Dr., Loop (312) 704-0655
160 W. Van Buren, Loop (312) 939-4208
202 N. Michigan Ave., Loop (312) 541-1313
225 N. Michigan Ave., Loop (312) 565-0009
227 W. Monroe St., Loop (312) 346-4360
231 S. LaSalle, Loop (312) 553-0373
400 W. Madison Ave., Loop (312) 975-2071
401 E. Ontario Ave., Loop (312) 951-7242
444 N. Michigan Ave, Loop (312) 832-9851
528 Dempster St., Evanston (847) 733-8328
555 S. Dearborn Ave., Loop (312) 922-8910
600 N. State St., Loop (312) 573-0033
617 W. Diversey, North (312) 880-5172
828 N. State St., Near North (312) 751-1676

932 N. Rush St., Near North (312) 951-5346
1001 W. Armitage, North (312) 528-1340
1018 Lake St., Oak Park (708) 848-5057
1023 W. Addison, North (312) 929-0945
1500 E. 53rd St., South (312) 324-1241
1533 N. Wells, Near North (312) 337-8899
2063 N. Clark, North (312) 525-6231
2114 Central St., Evanston (847) 328-1369
2200 N. Clyborn, North (312) 248-0908
2200 N. Halsted, North (312) 935-2622
2529 N. Clark, North (312) 296-0898
3358 N. Broadway Ave., North (312) 528-0343
3359 N. Southport, North (312) 975-2071
1724 Sherman Ave, Evanston (847) 492-0490

Third Coast Coffee House and Wine Bar

29 E. Deleware
Near North
(312) 664-7225
Su-Th 8 A.M.-1 A.M., F-Sa 8 A.M.-2 A.M.

$$$

Third Coast Coffee offers one of the biggest, tastiest menus with many eclectic salads, cold and hot sandwiches (including a roasted mushroom pesto), focaccia pizzas, and a long list of spirits, ports, sherries, red and white wines, and naturally, coffee and teas. A Gold Coast neighborhood favorite, it can get quite busy. However, the decor is elegant and subdued, and they offer a smoking section, and live music, and a nice neighborhood atmosphere. See coupon on page 146.

Third Coast Coffee House and Wine Bar

1260 N. Dearborn St.
Near North
(312) 649-0730
Daily 24 hours

$$$

The Dearborn location offers much of the same as the Deleware shop except they're open all hours. It's too loud for reading but great for talking, and the antique globes and signs and old hotel atmosphere add some fun. This cafe is typically busy, so you may have to wait for service, but the coffee is strong and hot and the menu is satisfying.

Torrefazione Italia 1/2

2200 N. Lincoln Ave.
North
(312) 477-6847
M-Th 7 A.M.-9 P.M., F-Sa 7 A.M.-10 P.M., Su 8 A.M.-8 P.M.

$$$

From the Bizarri family tradition going back three generations, this Italian coffee roasting company is committed to the entire sensual experience of coffee. The seven unique blends are named after regions in Italy, and the pastries are fresh and flaky. The apricot walls, natural wood tables, and Deruta ceramic create an elegant atmosphere, while local artwork and easy chairs add comfort to this Lincoln Park cafe. Brooding is discouraged; instead, Torrefazione emphasizes a refined, truly authentic Italian experience. See coupon on page 147.

Uncommon Ground

1214 W. Grace St.
North
(312) 929-3680
Su-Th 8 A.M.-11 P.M., F-Sa 8 A.M.-12 A.M.

$$$

This Wrigleyville cafe would have a five-cup rating if it weren't for the slow, albeit well-meaning table service. However, the coffee is outstanding, the cafe is comfortable and surprisingly spacious (despite limited seating). Wonderful for reading, talking, or games, Uncommon Ground presents their desserts on plates swirled with chocolate, and serves large gourmet drinks in bowls. They feature live music on the weekends, and if you sit outside in the summer, you can meet many of the neighborhood's dogs and their owners.

Other locations:
Harold Washington Library, 400 S. State St. (312) 322-2444
Chicago Cultural Center, 77 E. Randolph St. (312) 541-0077

If you want to improve your understanding, drink coffee.
—Sydney Smith

Unicorn Cafe

1/2

1723 Sherman Ave.
Evanston
(847) 332-2312
Daily 7:30 A.M.-11 P.M.

$$

One of the first cafes in downtown Evanston, the Unicorn is a favorite Northwestern student hangout. This spacious storefront offers a basic cafe menu with consistently good coffee and usually tasty light fare. They display wonderful art, while light jazz or classical music plays on the sound system. The service is quick and businesslike, and despite the perpetual crowd, seats are always available. Sit by the psychedelic fish tank along the back wall with your favorite book and a latte to find contentment. See coupon on page 148.

University of Chicago Coffee Shops

Classics Coffee Shop

1/2

1010 E. 59th St., 2nd floor
(312) 702-0177
M-Th 8 A.M.-5 P.M., F 8 A.M.-4:30 P.M. (closed Saturdays and Sundays)

$$

Get ready for plenty of heady discussion in this cafe, frequented mostly by graduate students and professors. With philosophical arguments in one corner, a music student practicing an instrument in another, and little space between tables, this shop is ideal for people watchers. Try the oatmeal cookies and soak up the conversations.

Cobb Hall Coffee Shop 1/2
5811 S. Ellis Ave. in the basement
(312) 702-9236
M-F 8:30 A.M.-4:30 P.M. (closed Saturdays and Sundays)

$$

Many students call this the best campus coffee shop. It certainly has the most extensive menu and is the only one to serve the revered Medici pizza for lunch. Although the lunch crowd of mostly undergraduates can make seating scarce, most other times you can usually find a seat to enjoy your book or conversation.

Divinity School Cafe 1/2
1025 E. 58th St. in the basement
(312) 702-7111
M-F 8 A.M.-4:30 P.M. (closed Saturdays and Sundays)

$

On first glance, you may think you have stumbled into someone's boiler room, but the Div is warm, cozy, and conversational. Offering dishes from various Hyde Park restaurants, a visitor can pick American, Thai, Indian, and other types of food, most of which are around $3 a plate and taste wonderful. The coffee can be inconsistent, but you can hang your own mug on the wall if you're a regular.

Ex Libris

1100 E. 57th St., A Level
(312) 702-7645
M-Th 8:30 A.M.-11:30 A.M., F 8:30 A.M.-6 P.M., Sa 11 A.M.-6 P.M., Su 12 P.M.-6 P.M.

$$$

A nice break from studies in the Regenstein Library, Ex Libris provides an outlet for students and outsiders alike. With a menu offering Indian and Middle Eastern foods, along with donuts and bagels, you can satisfy any craving. They serve only regular coffee here, and it's all-nighter, industrial-strength brew, but the cafe is spacious and great for people watching. No takeout orders are permitted.

Smart Museum Cafe

5550 S. Greenwood Ave.
(312) 702-0200
M-F 9 A.M.-4 P.M., Sa-Su 12 P.M.-5 P.M.

$1/2

Located within the contemporary art museum on campus, the Smart Museum Cafe is basically a cart surrounded by tables. The white formica tables and wire chairs reflect the artistic ambience, but otherwise the atmosphere is lacking. The offerings are typical cafe drinks and snacks, the coffee is good and a bargain at $1. If you're visiting the museum, stop by.

Weiss Coffee Shop

1116 E. 59th St.
South
(312) 667-9638
M-Th 9 A.M.-10:30 P.M., F 9 A.M.-5 P.M., Su 1 P.M.-10:30 P.M.
  (closed Saturdays)

$$$

Although Weiss lacks somewhat in atmosphere, it's a great place to come for a study break in the gorgeous old Harper Library. Although the air can be intense at times, especially with students panicking during exams, the coffee is good and the quiet location allows for plenty of reading.

Urbus Orbis 1/2

1934 W. North Ave.
West
(312) 252-4446
M-Sa 9 A.M.-12 A.M., Su 10 A.M.-12 A.M.

$$$

This Wicker Park gem has several flaws, including abrupt service, comparatively high prices, and inconsistent quality. However, the wonderful artsy atmosphere more than makes up for everything. With wood floors, exposed brick walls, and lots of local art, they provide a great place to read, talk, or meditate. If that's not your bag, a long wall of magazines welcomes you, as well as two Internet computers. The menu is eclectic and includes an assortment of drinks, breads, local desserts, cakes, salads, and vegetarian plates.

Verona   ☕☕☕☕1/2

1355 W. Wrightwood Ave.
North
(312) 935-0081
Tu-Th 5:30 P.M.-11 P.M., F 5:30 P.M.-12 A.M.,
     Sa-Su 8:30 A.M.-1 P.M., 5:30 P.M.-12 A.M.

$$

Tucked into the corner of Wrightwood and Wayne Streets, you'll find a small wine bar and cafe with an interior decor of plaster angels, vivid frescoes, and lots of candlelight. However, the atmosphere is not too artsy; Verona attracts a neighborhood crowd. The menu offers small gourmet dishes for very reasonable prices, and by the number of people ordering takeout, it has proved to be good. Sunday and Saturday brunch draws a loyal following, and the owner is extremely laid-back and friendly. The coffee is rich and strong and the wines are high quality. Verona is a surprising find in a residential neighborhood.

The average American's simplest and commonest form of breakfast
consists of coffee and beefsteak.
—Mark Twain, *A Tramp Abroad* (1879)

Victoria's Cafe

2444 N. Clark St.
North
(312) 528-8500
M-Th 10 A.M.-12 A.M., F-Sa 8 A.M.-2 A.M., Su 8 A.M.-10 P.M.

$$$

Located in one of the last three houses untouched by the Great Chicago Fire, Victoria's Cafe is the only multilevel Victorian coffeehouse in town. The period decor provides elegance while the comfortable seating and scattered games add comfort to this Lincoln Park cafe. The light fare to full meals are good, and the extensive coffee and tea offerings are wonderfully prepared. Call for information on their many presentations, including music, readings, and independent films. Victoria's is a great place to lose yourself for an afternoon or evening.

Viennese Kaffee-Haus Brandt 1/2

3423 N. Southport Ave.
North
(312) 528-2220
Tu-Th 7 A.M.-10 P.M.. F 7 A.M.-11 P.M., Sa 9 A.M.-11 P.M.,
    Su 9 A.M.-6 P.M. (closed Mondays)

$$-$$$

Tucked below the Ravenswood el, this quiet European shop may go unnoticed; however, it is worth a long visit. The back of the menu describes the painstaking effort to create the Old World atmosphere, which is complete with vintage 1920s jazz, huge antique glass cases, and marble as far as you can see. They roast their own coffee, make their own ice cream, and even prepare all of their desserts, including hard-to-find meringues for displaced New Yorkers. A full menu is available for more than a snack, and the outdoor seating in the summer is extremely popular. For outstanding coffee and tasty desserts, Kaffee-Haus Brandt is a must.

Waterstone's Bookstore Cafe

840 N. Michigan Ave.
Near North
(312) 751-9188
M-Sa 8 A.M.-9 P.M., Su 11 A.M.-6 P.M.

$$

This cafe plunked down into the middle of the bookstore has a counter and tables surrounded by books. Although this is a good place to browse over a book you're considering buying, it's not worth a visit on its own. They do offer beer and wine, as well as a drink called Caesar's Last Wish, which is a double espresso with a shot of sambuca.

Why Not Coffee House   1/2
1059 W. Belmont Ave.
North
(312) 404-2800
Daily 10 A.M.-1 A.M.

$1/2

This spacious and bright cafe attracts a lot of students and
groups for dessert and coffee. The table service is thorough, although the lone server is kept quite busy with a weeknight
crowd. However, the coffee is good and inexpensive, and a fire-
place adds warmth and character. A couple of annoyances, such
as $1 rent for cards or chess, used books strictly for sale, and re-
verberating group conversations, may dampen the charm. But,
as the name suggests, why not try it?

Wolf & Kettle Coffeehouse
51 E. Pearson St.
Near North
(312) 915-8595
M-Sa 6:30 A.M.-11:30 P.M., Su 9 A.M.-11:30 P.M.

$$$

The Wolf & Kettle is tucked behind several Loyola buildings
and is frequented by downtown students. The service is some-

what unresponsive and slow, but the cafe itself is soothing, with large wooden tables, long couches, reading materials, and Louis Armstrong playing overhead. The prices seem high, but the scones have wonderful traces of almond and the lattes stand with some of the best. A nice alternative to the chains, try this cafe after a Magnificent Mile shopping trip.

Go to the Source

Many of the coffee shops listed enjoy the wares of several of the following bakers and roasters. Try these outlets for a taste from the source.

Anna, Ida & Me
1117 W. Grand Ave.
Loop
(312) 243-2662
M-F 8 A.M.-5:30 P.M., Sa 10 A.M.-4 P.M. (closed Sundays)

A source of pastries for many of Chicago's coffeehouses and considered by many to have the best ruggelah in the area, Anna, Ida & Me is a tiny bakery west of the Loop. The trip is worth it, however, to try the fresh, tasty pastries. They specialize in custom gourmet gifts, and you can sip on complimentary coffee while you nibble on some treats.

Casteel & Company
801 Main St.
Evanston
(847) 733-1187
Tu-F 10 A.M.-6:30 P.M.; Sa 10 A.M.-5 P.M.

If you are looking for supplies—whether basic or exotic—for making coffee at home, try Casteel. Casteel's shelves hold unusual coffee makers, espresso machines, beans roasted on the premises. They have supplies for Chemex, a hard-to-find coffee maker cleaner, and gaskets for stovetop espresso makers. They sell great beans with good advice to go along, and they'll also sell you a coffee to go (no food). See coupon on page 122.

Coffee & Tea Exchange

3300 N. Broadway Ave.
North
(312) 528-2241
M-Th 7:30 A.M.-8 P.M., F 7:30 A.M. -7 P.M., Sa 9 A.M.-7 P.M.,
Su 10 A.M.-6 P.M.

The smell of spices and coffee wafts out when you walk by Coffee & Tea Exchange. Primarily a source for fresh-roasted beans (roasted in a Chicago warehouse), any supplies—from grinders and espresso makers to mugs and creamers—are available. As far as coffees go, they boast a selection of over thirty beans from which to choose. They also offer fresh coffee, muffins, scones, and cookies for the takeout visitor, but this is basically a home brewer's shop. They also supply coffee to many of Chicago's coffeehouses.

Other location:
833 W. Armitage Ave., North (312) 929-6730

Hayes Coffee

1010 North Blvd.
Oak Park
(708) 524-1914
M-F 7 A.M.-7 P.M., Sa 9 A.M.-6 P.M. (closed Sundays)

This Oak Park roastery offers beans, spices, oats, teas, and mixed herbs, but try the beans freshly roasted by Mr. Hayes himself. Stop in for supplies, or simply stop in; one deep breath is worth a double espresso. See coupon on page 133.

Maps

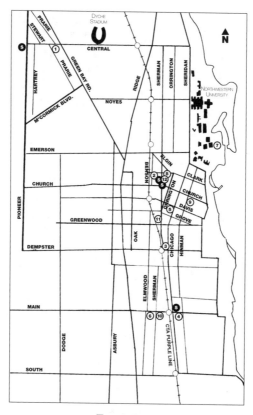

Evanston

1. Bean Counter Cafe
2. Cafe Ambiance
3. Cafe Express
4. Cafe Express South
5. Cafe Mozart Espresso Bar
6. Casteel & Company
7. Higher Ground

8. J. K. Sweets
9. Kafein
10. Mama Java's Cafe
11. The Opera Cafe
12. Unicorn Cafe

S. Starbucks location

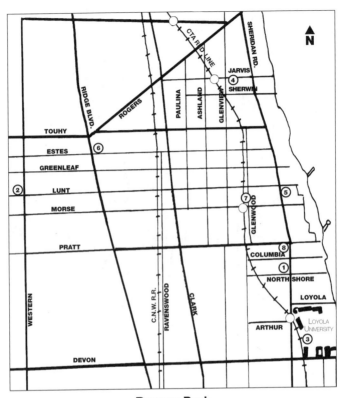

Rogers Park

1. Atomic Cafe
2. Bean Post
3. Brother's Coffee
4. Don's Coffee Club
5. Ennui Cafe
6. Hardboiled
7. No Exit Cafe
8. Panini Panini

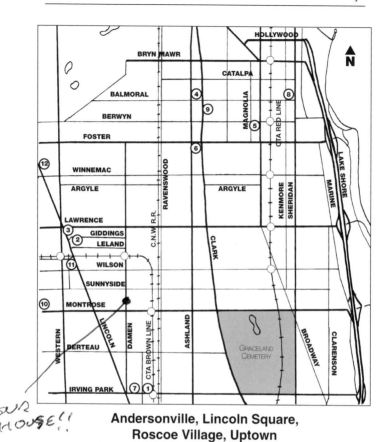

**Andersonville, Lincoln Square,
Roscoe Village, Uptown**

1. Café 28
2. Cafe Selmarie
3. Cafe Umbrella
4. Coffee Chicago
5. Coffee Chicago
6. Great Lakes Coffee and Tea
7. Grind & Brew Coffeehouse
8. Joe Mocha
9. Kopi, A Traveler's Cafe
10. Lutz Continental Cafe and Bakery
11. Nervous Center
12. Rok Coffee Emporium

Wrigleyville, Lakeview, North Lincoln Park

1. Bittersweet
2. Brother's Coffee
3. Cafe Avanti
4. Café Voltaire
5. Caffé Pergolesi
6. Casa Java
7. Coffee Chicago
8. Coffee Chicago
9. Coffee Chicago
10. Coffee & Tea Exchange
11. Corona's Coffee Shop
12. Emerald City Coffee Bar
13. Halsted Street Digital Audio Cafe
14. Intelligentsia
15. Interactive Bean
16. Island Java
17. Kokomo Caffe
18. la Madeleine
19. La Piazza Cafe
20. Lunar Cabaret and Full Moon Cafe
21. Mozart Cafe
22. Perk: A Drink House
23. Roscoe's Cafe
24. Scene's Coffee House and Dramatist Bookstore
25. Uncommon Ground
26. Viennese Kaffee Haus Brandt
27. Why Not Coffee House
S. Starbucks locations

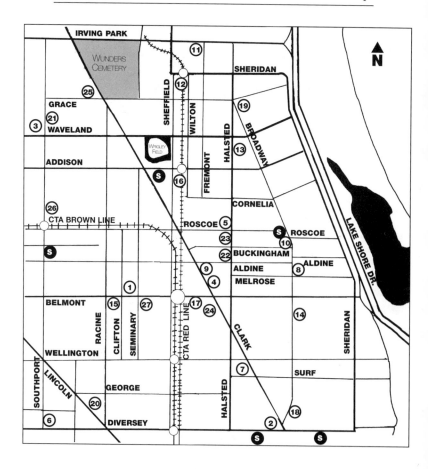

**Wrigleyville, Lakeview,
North Lincoln Park**

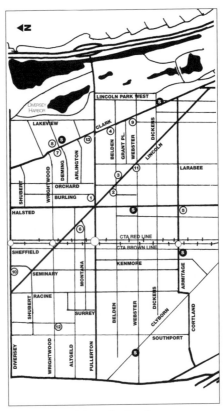

Lincoln Park

1. Bourgeois Pig!
2. Café Equinox
3. Caffe Trevi
4. Capra's Coffee
5. Coffee & Tea Exchange
6. Corby Coffee
7. Fonté Coffee Company
8. Gourmet Coffee Company
9. Java Centrale
10. Jazzy Cafe
11. Torrefazione Italia
12. Verona
13. Victoria's Cafe

S. Starbucks location

Gold Coast

1. Border's Coffee Shop
2. Boudin Bakery Cafe
3. Coffee Chicago
4. Espresso Pacifico
5. Gloria Jean's Coffee Beans
6. Godiva Chocolatier
7. Saint Germain Bakery
8. Savories

9. Third Coast Coffee
10. Third Coast Coffee House and Wine Bar
11. Waterstone's Bookstore Cafe
12. Wolf & Kettle Coffeehouse

S. Starbucks locations

River North/Loop

1. Artist's Cafe
2. au bon pain
3. au bon pain
4. au bon pain
5. au bon pain
6. au bon pain
7. au bon pain
8. Brewster's Coffee Co.
9. Brewster's Coffee Co.
10. Brewster's Coffee Co.
11. Brother's Coffee
12. Cafe de Case
13. Cafe Josephine
14. Caffe Baci
15. Caffe Baci
16. Caffe Classico
17. Caffe Classico
18. Caffe Classico
19. Cream City Cafe
20. Fonté Coffee Company
21. Gloria Jean's
22. Gloria Jean's
23. Gloria Jean's
24. Gloria Jean's
25. Gloria Jean's
26. Gloria Jean's
27. Gourmand Coffeehouse
28. Gourmet Cup Coffee
29. Gourmet Cup Coffee
30. Gourmet Cup Coffee
31. Jacobs Brothers Java
32. Krystyna's Cafe
33. Liberty Coffee & Teas
34. Metro Espresso
35. Seattle's Best Coffee

36. Seattle's Best Coffee
37. Uncommon Ground
38. Uncommon Ground

S. Starbucks locations

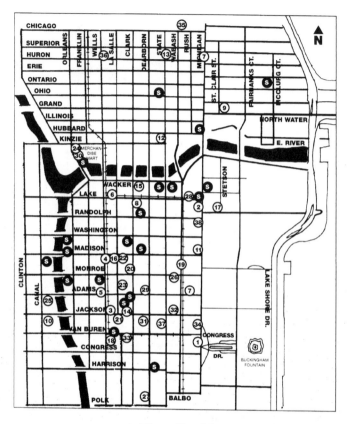

**River North/
Loop**

Hyde Park

1. Caffé Florian
2. Emma G's
3. Medici
4. Ex Libris
5. Weiss
6. Classics
7. Divinity
8. Cobb Hall
9. Smart Museum

S. Starbucks locations

indexes

Index by Location

Espresso Pacifico
Saint Germain Bakery
Starbucks
Third Coast Coffee House
    and Wine Bar
Waterstone's Bookstore Cafe
Wolf & Kettle Coffeehouse

Hyde Park

53rd Street south to 60th,
between Cottage Grove and
Stony Island

Caffé Florian
Emma G's
Medici
Starbucks
University of Chicago
    Classics Coffee Shop
    Cobb Hall
    Divinity School
    Ex Libris
    Smart Museum Cafe
    Weiss Coffee Shop

Lakeview

Belmont north to Irving Park
Road, east of Ravenswood

Bittersweet
Cafe Avanti
Café Voltaire

Caffé Pergolesi
Coffee & Tea Exchange
Coffee Chicago
Corona's Coffee Shop
Emerald City Coffee Bar
Halsted Street Digital Audio
    Cafe
Interactive Bean
Island Java
Kokomo Caffe
La Piazza Cafe
Mozart Cafe
Perk: A Drink House
Roscoe's Cafe
Scenes Coffee House and
    Dramatist Bookstore
Starbucks
Uncommon Ground
Viennese Kaffee Haus
    Brandt
Why Not Coffee House

Lincoln Park

Armitage north to Belmont, east
of Ashland

Bourgeois Pig!
Brother's Coffee
Café Equinox
Caffe Trevi
Capra's Coffee
Casa Java
Coffee & Tea Exchange

Uncommon Ground (in the
Chicago Cultural Center)

Oak Park

Hayes Coffee
Java Joans
Some Things Brewing
Starbucks

Old Irving Park
*West of Cicero on Irving Park
Road*

Java Thai

River North
*Chicago Avenue south to the
river, east of Orleans*

Brewster's Coffee Co.
Cafe de Casa
Cafe Josephine
Gloria Jean's Coffee Beans
Godiva Chocolatier
Seattle's Best Coffee
Starbucks

River West
*Chicago Avenue south to the
river, between Orleans and
Racine*

Anna, Ida & Me
Damato's House of Coffee
Little Miss Muffin

Rogers Park
*Devon north to Howard,
Western east to the lake*

Atomic Cafe
Bean Post
Brother's Coffee
Don's Coffee Club
Ennui Cafe
Hardboiled
No Exit Cafe
Panini Panini

Roscoe Village
*Belmont north to Irving Park
Road, between Ravenswood and
I-94*

Café 28
Grind & Brew Coffeehouse
Higher Ground

South Loop
Madison south to Polk, east of the river

Artist's Cafe
au bon pain
Brother's Coffee
Caffe Baci
Caffe Classico
Cream City Cafe
Fonté Coffee Company
Gloria Jean's Coffee Beans
Gourmand Coffeehouse
Gourmet Cup Coffee
Jacobs Bros. Java
Krystyna's Cafe

Liberty Coffee and Teas
Metro Espresso
Starbucks
Uncommon Ground (in the
    Harold Washington
    Library)

South Side
Polk south to the city limits, except for Hyde Park, Beverly, and Chinatown

Beanie's Coffee & Tea Shoppe
Cafe Jumping Bean

Index of Special Features

smoking is permitted or smoking section is available

Artist's Cafe
Bean Counter Cafe
Bourgeois Pig!
Cafe Cappuccino
Cafe Express
Cafe Jumping Bean
Cafe Umbrella
Cafe Voltaire
Caffe Florian
Caffe Latte
Caffe Pergolesi
Caffe Trevi
Coffee Chicago
Corona's Coffee Shop
Damato's House of Coffee
Don's Coffee Club
Earwax Cafe
Ennui Cafe
Garson's Gourmet Coffee Cafe
Grind & Brew Coffeehouse
Jamoch's Caffe Ltd.
Java Express
Kafein
Kokomo Caffe
Kopi, A Traveler's Cafe
La Piazza

Logan Beach
Lunar Cabaret and Full Moon Cafe
Mama's Paradise Cafe
Medici
Nervous Center
No Exit Cafe
Perk: A Drink House
Roscoe's Coffeehouse
Saint Germain Bakery
Scenes Coffee House and Dramatist Bookstore
Third Coast Coffee House and Wine Bar
Urbus Orbis
Victoria's Cafe
Viennese Kaffee-Haus Brandt
Why Not Coffee House

outdoor seating in nice weather

Artist's Cafe
Atomic Cafe
Bean Counter Cafe
Beverly Bean
Brewster's Coffee Company
Cafe Avanti
Cafe Express
Cafe Express South

 **couches**

artwork on display

live music

Lunar Cabaret and Full Moon
  Cafe
Mad Bar & Cafe
Mama Java's Cafe
Mozart Cafe
No Exit Cafe
Opera Cafe
Rok Coffee Emporium
Roscoe's Coffeehouse
Third Coast Coffee House
  and Wine Bar
Uncommon Ground
Victoria's Cafe

 **live readings—
poetry, comedy,
skits,
performance art**

Beanie's Coffee & Tea Shoppe
Bittersweet
Cafe Jumping Bean
Cafe Luna
Cafe Voltaire
Caffe Trevi
Espresso Pacifico
Grind & Brew Coffeehouse
Kafein
La Piazza
Lunar Cabaret and Full Moon
  Cafe
No Exit Cafe

Scenes Coffee House and
  Dramatist Bookstore
Urbus Orbis
Victoria's Cafe

 table games

Atomic Cafe
Beanie's Coffee & Tea Shoppe
Beverly Bean
Bourgeois Pig!
Cafe Equinox
Cafe Jumping Bean
Cafe Luna
Caffe Trevi
Earwax Cafe
Emerald City Coffee Bar
Espresso Pacifico
Garson's Gourmet Coffee Cafe
Grind & Brew Coffeehouse
Halsted Street Digital Audio
  Cafe
Hardboiled
Interactive Bean
Island Java
Kafein
Kokomo Caffe
La Piazza
Nervous Center
No Exit Cafe
Some Things Brewing
Victoria's Cafe

books to read/books to buy

Bean Counter Cafe
Beverly Bean
Borders Coffee Shop
Bourgeois Pig!
Cafe Jumping Bean
Cafe Luna
Cafe Mozart Espresso Bar
Great Lakes Coffee and Tea, Ltd.
Grind & Brew Coffeehouse
Hardboiled
Higher Ground (Northwest)
Interactive Bean
Kopi, A Traveler's Cafe
La Piazza
No Exit Cafe
Savories
Some Things Brewing
Waterstone's Bookstore Cafe

beer and wine also served

Artist's Cafe
Cafe Cappuccino
Cafe Umbrella
Cafe Voltaire
Caffe Latte
Gourmand Coffeehouse
La Piazza
Lutz Continental Cafe and Pastry Shop
Mad Bar & Cafe
Roscoe's Coffeehouse
Saint Germain Bakery
Third Coast Coffee House and Wine Bar
Verona
Viennese Kaffee-Haus Brandt
Waterstone's Bookstore Cafe

Index by Rating

Island Java
Java Express
Java Joans
Kopi, A Traveler's Cafe
Krystyna's Cafe
Logan Beach
Mad Bar and Cafe
Mama Java's Cafe
Medici
Mozart Cafe
Opera Cafe
Panini Panini
Rok Coffee Emporium
Roscoe's Coffeehouse
Saint Germain Bakery
Scenes Coffee House and
    Dramatist Bookstore
Third Coast Coffee House
    and Wine Bar (both loca-
    tions)
Wolf & Kettle Coffeehouse

☕☕☕1/2

Brewster's Coffee Co.
Brother's Gourmet Coffee
Cafe Ambiance
Cafe Josephine
Cafe Mozart Espresso Bar
Cafe 28
Cafe Umbrella
Cappuccino Alfredo
Coffee Chicago

Corona's Coffee Shop
Earwax Cafe
Ennui Cafe
Fonte Coffee Company
Garson's Gourmet Coffee Cafe
Jacobs Bros. Java
Jamoch's Caffe Ltd.
Lutz Continental Cafe and
    Pastry Shop
Classics Coffee Shop (Univer-
    sity of Chicago)
Cobb Hall Coffee Shop (Uni-
    versity of Chicago)
Why Not Coffee House

☕☕☕

Artist's Cafe
Beanie's Coffee and Tea
    Shoppe
Cafe Cafina
Cafe Luna
Caffe Latte
Capra's Coffee
Corby Coffee
Emma G's
Espresso Pacifico
Gloria Jean's Coffee Beans
Godiva Chocolatier
Higher Ground (Northwest-
    ern University)
Java Centrale
La Madeleine
Liberty Coffee & Teas

Coupon Passport

Here's where you'll find some free coffee and snacks from many of the coffeehouses in this book. To redeem the coupons, you must follow these steps:

1. Bring this book to the coffee shop and present it to the counter help when you place your order. **Do not tear the coupons out of the book**.
2. The coffee shop will redeem your coupon by stamping it with their Coffee Lover's Chicago stamp or a stamp of their own.

You can use the space within each coupon to write notes, make your own mini review, catch an anecdote, or record your thoughts. Or simply leave it blank. Your passport becomes a memento of where you've been and what you've had to eat and drink on your coffee tour through Chicago. We hope each visit is a pleasurable and memorable one.

6746 N. Sheridan Rd.
(312) 764-9988

Get one free muffin or scone
with purchase of one regular
cafe latte or cafe mocha

Expires May 31, 1997

Coupon void if removed from book. No photocopies accepted.

1932 Central Street
Evanston
(847) 332-1116

Buy one expresso drink, get one free
(cappuccino, mocha, espresso, iced cappuccino,
iced mocha, latte, cap shake, mocha shake, etc.)

Expires May 31, 1997

Coupon void if removed from book. No photocopies accepted.

The Bean Post

2404 W. Lunt Ave.
(312) 338-7700

$2.00 off any
pound purchase

Expires May 31, 1997

Coupon void if removed from book. No photocopies accepted.

BEANIE'S
COFFEE &
TEA
SHOPPE

7150 S. Exchange Ave.
(312) 734-7699

Good for one large cup of the special coffee of the day

Expires May 31, 1997

STAMP
HERE

2734 W. 111th St.
(312) 239-6688

Bring a Friend Special
Buy one sandwich and beverage, get
one sandwich and beverage of equal
or lesser value free

Expires May 31, 1997

Coupon void if removed from book. No photocopies accepted.

900 N. Michigan Ave.
(312) 649-3570

One free muffin or pastry with the purchase of any espresso drink

Expires May 31, 1997

Coupon void if removed from book. No photocopies accepted.

Bourgeois Pig!

738 W. Fullerton Ave.
(312) 883-JAVA

Good for one large cup of daily brew
or one free regular latte
or cappuccino

Expires May 31, 1997

Coupon void if removed from book. No photocopies accepted.

3706 N. Southport Ave.
(312) 880-5959

Good for one large cup of the special coffee of the day

Expires May 31, 1997

Coupon void if removed from book. No photocopies accepted.

CAFE

1588 N. Milwaukee Ave.
(312) 227-8400

One complimentary latte, cappuccino, or coffee

Expires May 31, 1997

Coupon void if removed from book. No photocopies accepted.

STAMP
HERE

1439 W. 18th St.
(312) 455-0019

Get one free muffin or scone with the purchase of one regular cafe latte or cafe mocha

Expires May 31, 1997

2327 W. Giddings Ave.
(312) 989-5595

Get one free muffin or scone with the purchase of a regular cafe latte or regular cappuccino

Expires May 31, 1997

2308 N. Clark St.
(312) 665-7182

One free regular cafe latte

Expires May 31, 1997

Coupon void if removed from book. No photocopies accepted.

801 Main St.
(847) 733-1187

One free regular
cafe latte

Expires May 31, 1997

Coupon void if removed from book. No photocopies accepted.

Damato's

1123 W. Grand Ave.
(312) 733-5488

Good for one large cappuccino

Expires May 31, 1997

Coupon void if removed from book. No photocopies accepted.

1439 W. Jarvin Ave.
(312) 274-1228

Free coffee (bottomless cup)
with purchase of any food item
($2.00 or more)

Expires May 31, 1997

3928 N. Sheridan Rd.
(312) 525-7847

Free grande
beverages for two

Expires May 31, 1997

Coupon void if removed from book. No photocopies accepted.

835 N. Michigan Ave.
Water Tower Place
(312) 994-7767

$2.00 off one pound of coffee
Bring this coupon to our Water Tower Store and
receive $2.00 off a pound of any of our 48 different
coffees from around the world. Not valid with
any other coffee on sale.

Expires May 31, 1997

Coupon void if removed from book. No photocopies accepted.

835 N. Michigan Ave.
Water Tower Place
(312) 994-7767

Free second drink with this coupon
at our Water Tower Store when you buy the first
drink at regular price. Free drink must be
of equal or lesser value.

Expires May 31, 1997

Coupon void if removed from book. No photocopies accepted.

GODIVA
Chocolatier

835 N. Michigan Ave.
Water Tower Place
(312) 280-1133

One free biscotti with the purchase of any coffee item

Expires May 31, 1997

gourmand
coffeehouse

728 S. Dearborn Ave.
(312) 427-2610

Get one free muffin or scone with purchase of one regular cafe latte or cafe mocha

Expires May 31, 1997

Coupon void if removed from book. No photocopies accepted.

THE
GRIND & BREW
COFFEEHOUSE

1920 W. Irving Park Rd.
(312) 348-7592

One free cup of java

Expires May 31, 1997

Coupon void if removed from book. No photocopies accepted.

3641 N. Halsted Ave.
(312) 325-CAFE

Free (regular size) coffee, latte, or cappuccino
Offer not available for take out.

Expires May 31, 1997

Coupon void if removed from book. No photocopies accepted.

500 W. Madison
(312) 648-0070

Good for one free 16 oz. coffee
(house blend or flavor of the day)

Expires May 31, 1997

"Hayes"
Provisioners Gourmet
Since 1787

1010 North Blvd.
Oak Park
(708) 524-1914

One-quarter pound pure Hawaiian Kona per customer with this ad

No reproductions . . . must be original ad . . .

Expires December 29, 1996

2022 W. Roscoe
(312) 868-0075

Get one free muffin or scone with the purchase of one regular cafe latte or cafe mocha

Expires May 31, 1997

Coupon void if removed from book. No photocopies accepted.

3123 N. Broadway Ave.
(312) 348-8058

Get one large cup of the
special coffee of the day

Expires May 31, 1997

Coupon void if removed from book. No photocopies accepted.

Interactive**Bean**

1137 W. Belmont Ave.
(312) 528-2996

Good for one large cup of the special coffee of the day and 15% off computer rental

Expires May 31, 1997

Coupon void if removed from book. No photocopies accepted.

947 W. Addison
(312) 525-0299

Good for one large cup of the special coffee of the day

Expires May 31, 1997

Coupon void if removed from book. No photocopies accepted.

10701 S. Hale St.
(312) 233-8557

Good for one large cup of the
special coffee of the day

Expires May 31, 1997

Coupon void if removed from book. No photocopies accepted.

1621 Chicago Ave.
Evanston
(847) 491-1621

Buy one espresso drink, get one free
(cappuccino, mocha, latte, espresso, iced cap, iced mocha, cap shake, mocha shake, etc.)

Expires May 31, 1997

Coupon void if removed from book. No photocopies accepted.

5317 N. Clark St.
(312) 989-5674

One free regular espresso, cappuccino, or latte

Expires May 31, 1997

Coupon void if removed from book. No photocopies accepted.

3845 N. Broadway Ave.
(312) 868-0998

Good for one large cup of the
special coffee of the day

Expires May 31, 1997

Coupon void if removed from book. No photocopies accepted.

NO EXIT

CAFE/GALLERY

**6970 N. Glenwood Ave.
(312) 743-3355**

One free
regular cafe latte

Expires May 31, 1997

Coupon void if removed from book. No photocopies accepted.

Mozart Cafe

3727 N. Southport Ave.
(312) 348-1253

Get one coffee drink of any kind with the purchase of a drink at the same or greater value

Expires May 31, 1997

Coupon void if removed from book. No photocopies accepted.

STAMP
HERE

1458 Sherman Ave.
Evanston
(847) 332-2742

One free
regular cafe latte

Expires May 31, 1997

Coupon void if removed from book. No photocopies accepted.

3168 N. Clark St.
(312) 525-1007

Good for one free cappuccino with book or sandwich purchase

Expires May 31, 1997

Coupon void if removed from book. No photocopies accepted.

The Third Coast

29 E. Deleware Place
(312) 664-7225

Get one free scone with the purchase of one regular cafe latte or cafe mocha

Expires May 31, 1997

Coupon void if removed from book. No photocopies accepted.

STAMP
HERE

2200 N. Lincoln Ave.
(312) 477-6847

Good for one 8 oz. espresso drink or fresh-brewed coffee—free!

Expires May 31, 1997

Coupon void if removed from book. No photocopies accepted.

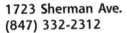

1723 Sherman Ave.
(847) 332-2312

One free regular cafe latte

Expires May 31, 1997

Coupon void if removed from book. No photocopies accepted.